Poetic Bipolar Mind
*Unraveling Life's Threads
Through Art and Words*

Written by Kiana Jimenez
Illustrated by David White

Poetic Bipolar Mind

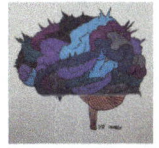

Copyright © 2024 Poetic Bipolar Mind

All rights reserved

The characters and events portrayed in this book are fictitious. Any similarity to real persons, living or dead, is coincidental and not intended by the author, Kiana Jimenez, and the illustrator, David White.

No part of this book may be reproduced, or stored in a retrieval system, or transmitted in any form or by any means, electronic, mechanical, photocopying, recording, or otherwise, without express written permission of the publisher, Poetic Bipolar Mind.

ISBN: 9798302702616

Cover design by: David White
Printed in the United States of America

To those who journey through darkness seeking light, the silent fighters and the souls who dare to hope. This book is dedicated to you.

May these words offer solace, understanding, and the courage to keep moving forward.

To my daughter, Khaleesi, your brief yet profound presence forever shaped my heart.
Your light guides me even on the darkest days, and this is for you—always.

And to David, thank you for sharing this creative path with me. Your art has brought these pages to life, and your belief in this vision means everything.

CONTENTS

Title Page
Copyright
Dedication
Night Ritual   1
"Ghost Ship"   2
Darkness Descends   4
"Distant Planet"   5
Self-Worth   7
"Sell Yourself"   9
Blank Canvas   11
"Blank Canvas"   14
Sunset Love   16
"Serenity"   18
Blind Love   20
"Pieces"   21
Drowning In Deadlines   23
"Time Crunch"   25
Lotus   27
"Lotus"   29
I Am Your Disease   31

"Self-Growth"	37
Love Unveiled	39
"Stop & Go"	40
Warped and Twisted	42
"FACEFEAR"	44
If Fate Were Kinder	46
"Psychedelic Sunflower"	47
Black Rose	49
"Black Rose"	51
Loving You, Losing Me	53
"Cruising"	55
Race	57
"Demolition"	61
Invisible Thread	63
"Fantasy Nightscape"	64
Love's True Muse	66
"The All Knowing"	67
Broken Promise	69
"302"	73
My Door's Key	75
"Home Is Where the Heart Is"	79
Hooded Figure	81
"Rock the Dragon"	84
ABOUT THE AUTHOR	86
Gallery of Works by David White	87
Author's note	89
Resources and Support	90

NIGHT RITUAL

Around, all around, the storm clouds gather.

My dread grows as the stroke of death falls against my naked soul.

It crushes me, and darkly my essence drips to

the cold, uncaring tombstones.

In abject fear, I begged for forgiveness,

while death loomed over me.

Now alone, my soul falls upon darkened eyes.

This is my doom.

"GHOST SHIP"

July 1, 2024

Drifting silently across an endless, shadowed sea, this spectral vessel seems caught in a liminal space between reality and the ethereal. The ship itself is weathered, its tattered sails and creaking hull steeped in history and haunting mystery. Pale, ghostly hues of gray and silver intermingle with faint streaks of deep blue, creating an atmosphere that feels both mournful and timeless.

The surrounding waters are deceptively calm, their surface rippling with an otherworldly glow that hints at hidden depths. The absence of a visible crew lends an eerie solitude to the scene, as though the ship carries the weight of forgotten stories, their echoes lingering in the air.

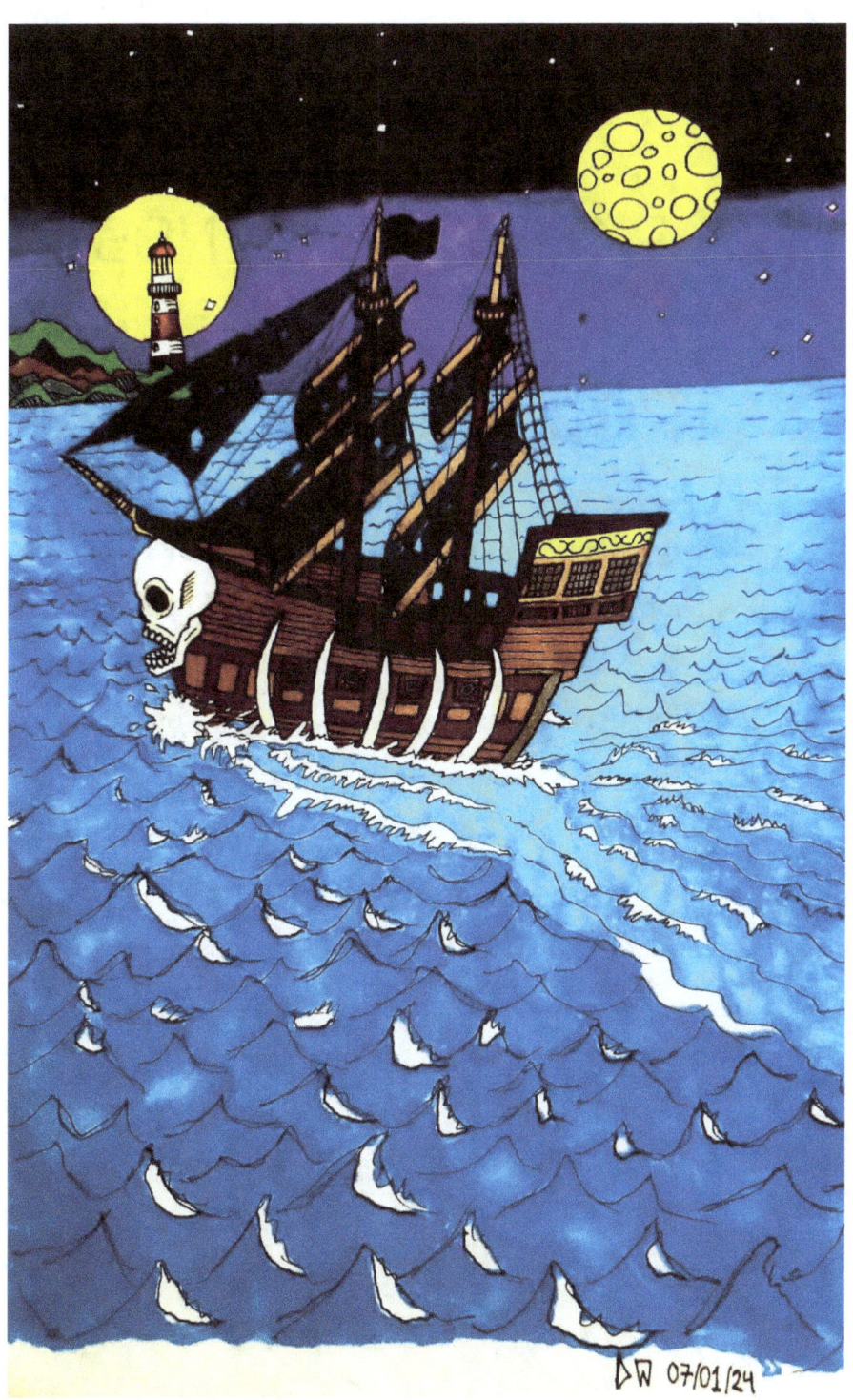

DARKNESS DESCENDS

The night falls in a heavy, suffocating cloak.
Entwined are we the salvation for which
you sacrificed yourself?
It flared once, but then it died, because of your obsession.
All hope must end. Your passion throbs no more.
How could you fail to believe?
Spir'its surround us, crying, we have lost our way.

"DISTANT PLANET"

October 1, 2024

Step into the ethereal unknown with a piece that feels like the first glimpse of an uncharted world. Shimmering gradients of turquoise, deep plum, and fiery gold swirl across a textured expanse, creating the illusion of a vast, otherworldly landscape. The alien terrain undulates with rolling curves and jagged peaks, simultaneously inviting exploration and caution.

This world is quiet, yet it hums with a silent vitality, as if its secrets are not just waiting to be uncovered but daring you to reveal them. The atmosphere is thick with the possibility of life unseen, life so different from our own that it defies comprehension. Shadows linger in the distance, suggestive of forms that may never fully come into focus, leaving the imagination to weave its own tales.

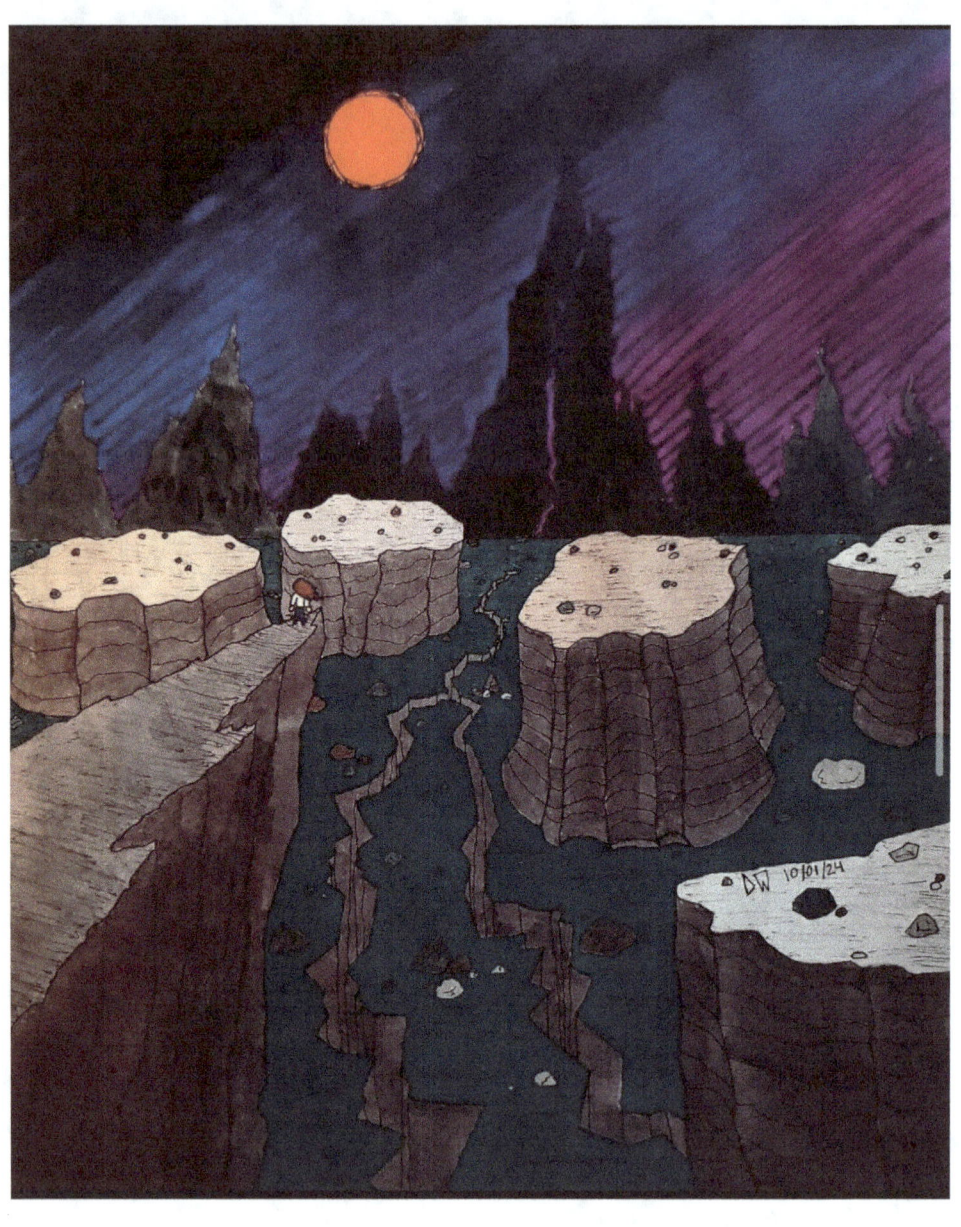

SELF-WORTH

Lately, I feel worthless.
I needed to find some value in me,
So I sold what I had
For little a fee.

My eyes for a penny
I sold to some fools,
They're blind and useless,
Mistook for jewels.

My lips for a nickel
To the sweetest sin,
So they'll know the love
That has never been.

My ears for a dime
I sold to a lover.
To hear sweet nothings,
And silence uncover.

My hands for a quarter
I sold to a ghost,
So that she might feel
What I've wanted the most.

Finally my bones for a dollar
I sold to the earth,
But as for my soul-
There was found no worth.

"SELL YOURSELF"

July 1, 2024

A stark and thought-provoking commentary on commodification, this piece combines fragmented elements of the human form eyes, lips, an ear, a hand with symbols of currency, such as coins and dollar bills. The skeletal bone at the center anchors the composition, evoking a sense of vulnerability and the stripping down of identity to its most basic value.

Each element feels detached yet connected, highlighting the tension between individuality and societal expectations. The handwritten words "Yourself Short" underscore the theme, serving as both a critique and a reminder of the cost of undervaluing one's worth.

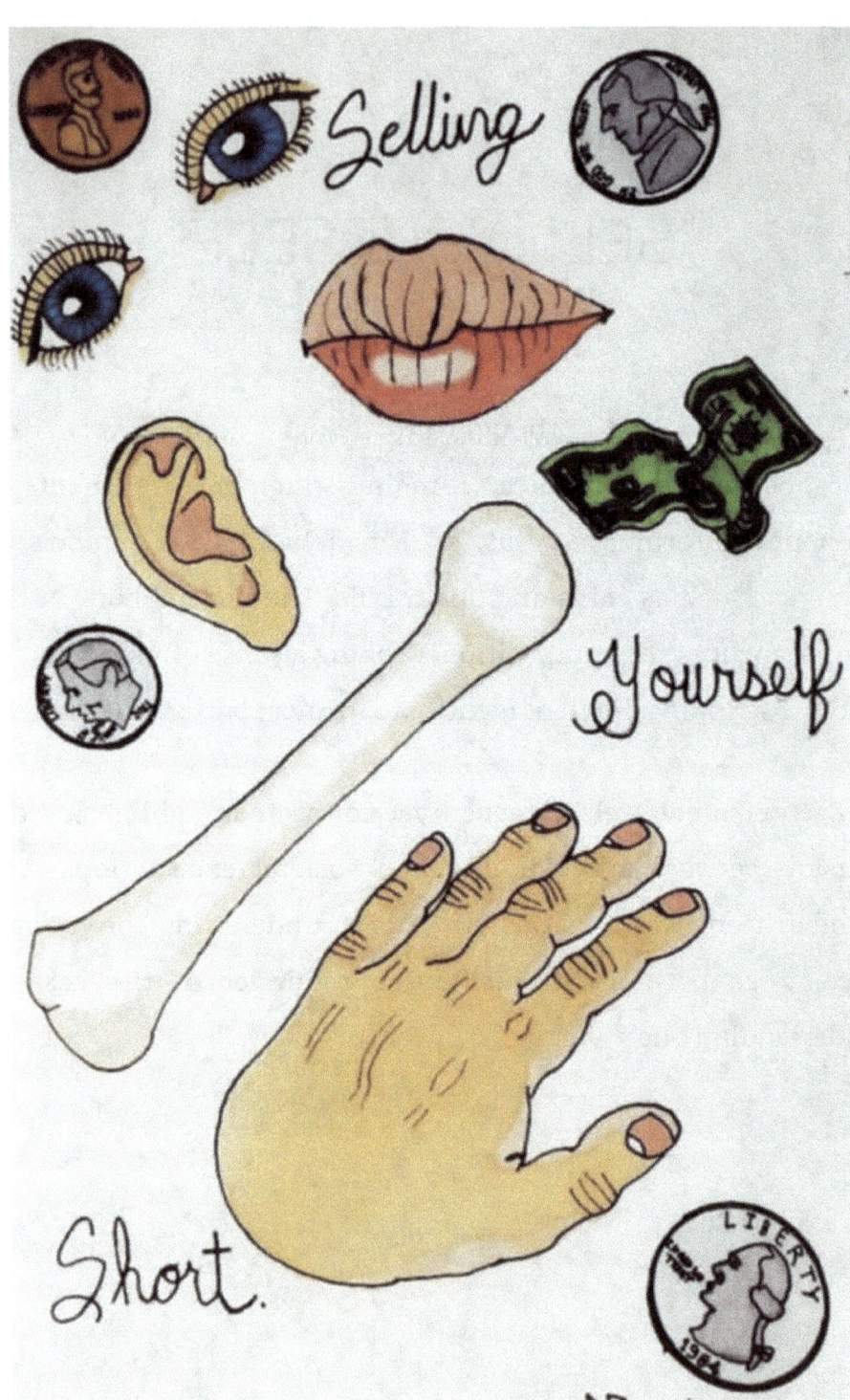

BLANK CANVAS

So many thoughts, so many ideas—
Yet my mind is a void, unfulfilled.
Like a painting waiting to come alive,
A masterpiece left still.

I yearn for beauty, for colors to burst,
To light this shadowed world I see.
But my mind is an expanse of white,
Racing like a storm endlessly.

My senses are dulled, yet I feel it all,
A paradox I cannot define.
I see what could be, what might exist,
Yet I'm stuck within the confines.

I am happy, I am sad,
I am angry, I am still.
I am nothing, I am blank,
A vessel yearning to be filled.

I miss the colors, the golden hues,
Of a sunrise warm and bright.
The deep blue waves of a quiet sea,
Whispering secrets at night.

I long for the red of a blooming rose,
Its petals, soft yet bold.
The tender green of springtime leaves,
Dancing where stories unfold.

I crave lavender skies at twilight's peak,
A canvas painted by the sun.
The rich brown earth beneath my feet,
Grounding me as dreams come undone.

I want the white of untouched snow,
Pure as it graces the ground.
The playful orange of autumn's leaves,
In their gentle, whirling sound.

I want it all back, I want to feel,
I want to fight, though I'm so tired.
The canvas waits, silent and patient,
For a moment yet inspired.

I imagine strokes, both delicate and bold,
Each one a whisper, giving life.
The artist's hand, both steady and wild,
Transforming darkness into light.

And in my stillness, I start to see—
I am the artist of my design.
With every breath, I fill the void,
With colors vibrant, bold, divine.

The final stroke completes the piece,
A vivid story, strong and bright.
The canvas, once empty, now sings with life,
A testament to my fight.

"BLANK CANVAS"

July 8, 2024

A breathtaking ode to potential, this piece is far from static despite its title. What begins as a stark white expanse quickly reveals subtle layers upon closer inspection. Wisps of color—barely visible—swirl at the edges, teasing at what could be. The void isn't emptiness; it's a realm brimming with untapped creativity, vibrating with a restless energy that feels as though it could burst forth at any moment.

The interplay of shadows across the canvas creates depth, evoking the swirling emotions that accompany the act of creation: fear, hope, exhilaration, doubt. This is not a passive canvas—it is alive with the push and pull of what is yet to come.

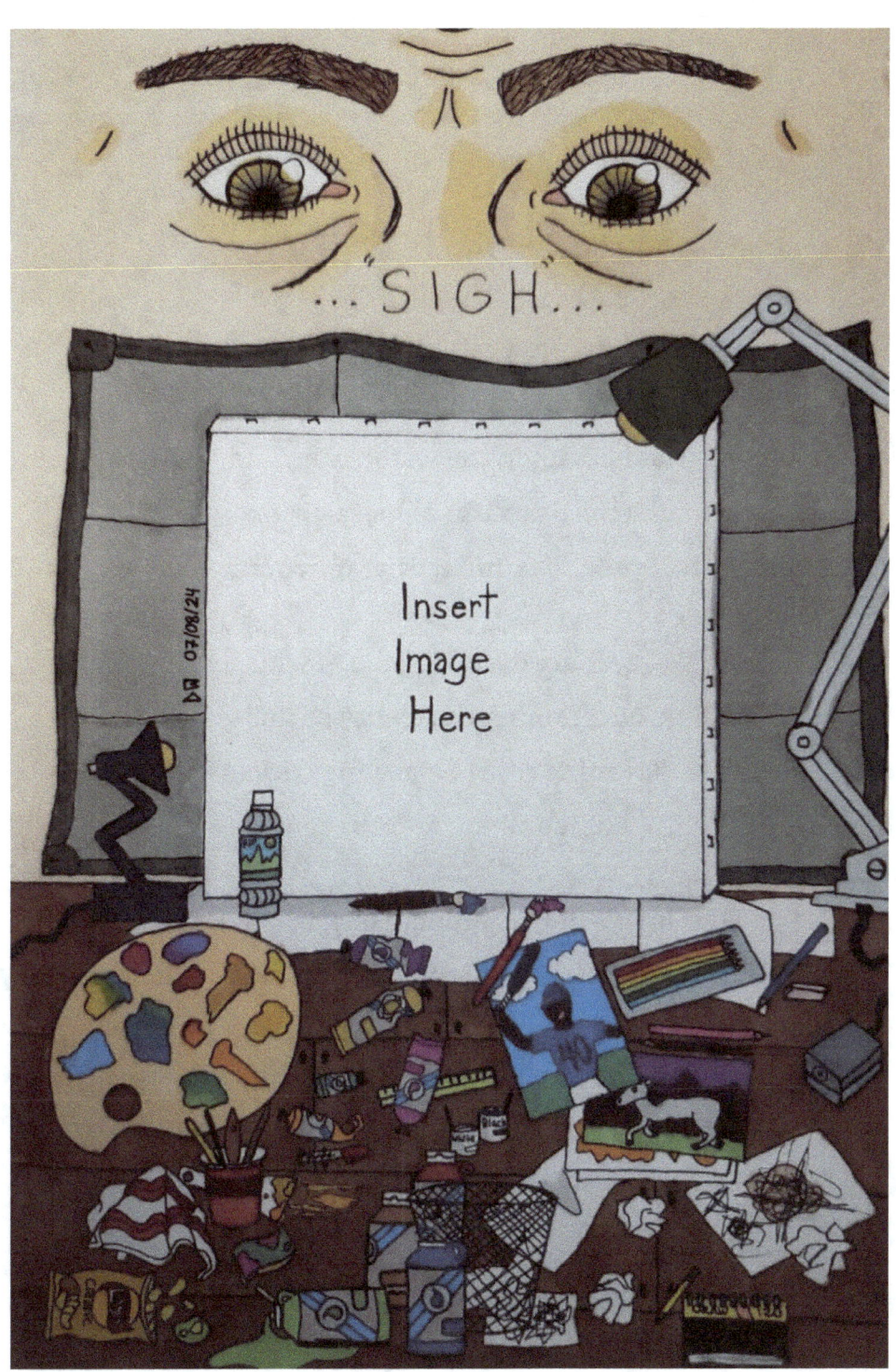

SUNSET LOVE

The sun is setting slowly, sinking beyond the horizon,
draping the sky in warm hues of orange and gold.
Its glow dances upon the water, calm and endless.
As I watch the beautiful scene, a vision unfolds.
It's you, with a smile so familiar, that mirrors the setting sun.

"My eyes are deceiving me," I whisper.
I blink, questioning the reality of this vision.
"My mind must be playing tricks."
But it's all too vivid to deny.

Your image lingers, undeniable, unwavering.
The sky being painted with the final blush of day,
A canvas of peace, made perfect by your presence.
Your arms are open, calling out, drawing me near.

Your voice is as gentle as the breeze.
Each word a whisper speaking of eternity,
I stay frozen, bound by the quiet air.
Suddenly, you stand before me, only a few inches away.

You whisper words of love, of timeless waiting.
The world fades around us, leaving only this moment.
In the quiet, I feel the weight of our eternity.

I knew it was time for me to go with you.
You reach me, your touch as real as the earth beneath us.
Hand in hand, we walk into the sunset's embrace,
where time stands still, and our love lives forever.

"SERENITY"

May 9, 2024

A visual lullaby, this piece envelops viewers in an embrace of tranquility. Soft gradients of pastel blue, lavender, and pale gold blend seamlessly, conjuring the image of dawn breaking over a still lake. Each curve and contour flows effortlessly into the next, evoking the feeling of a gentle breeze caressing the skin or the rhythmic lapping of water against a shore.

This is a sanctuary made visual—a place where burdens dissipate and time ceases to matter. Amid the harmony of colors and shapes, faint, organic patterns emerge, like the ripples of water disturbed only by a falling leaf. The illustration seems to breathe, whispering to its audience the timeless wisdom of nature: in stillness, there is strength.

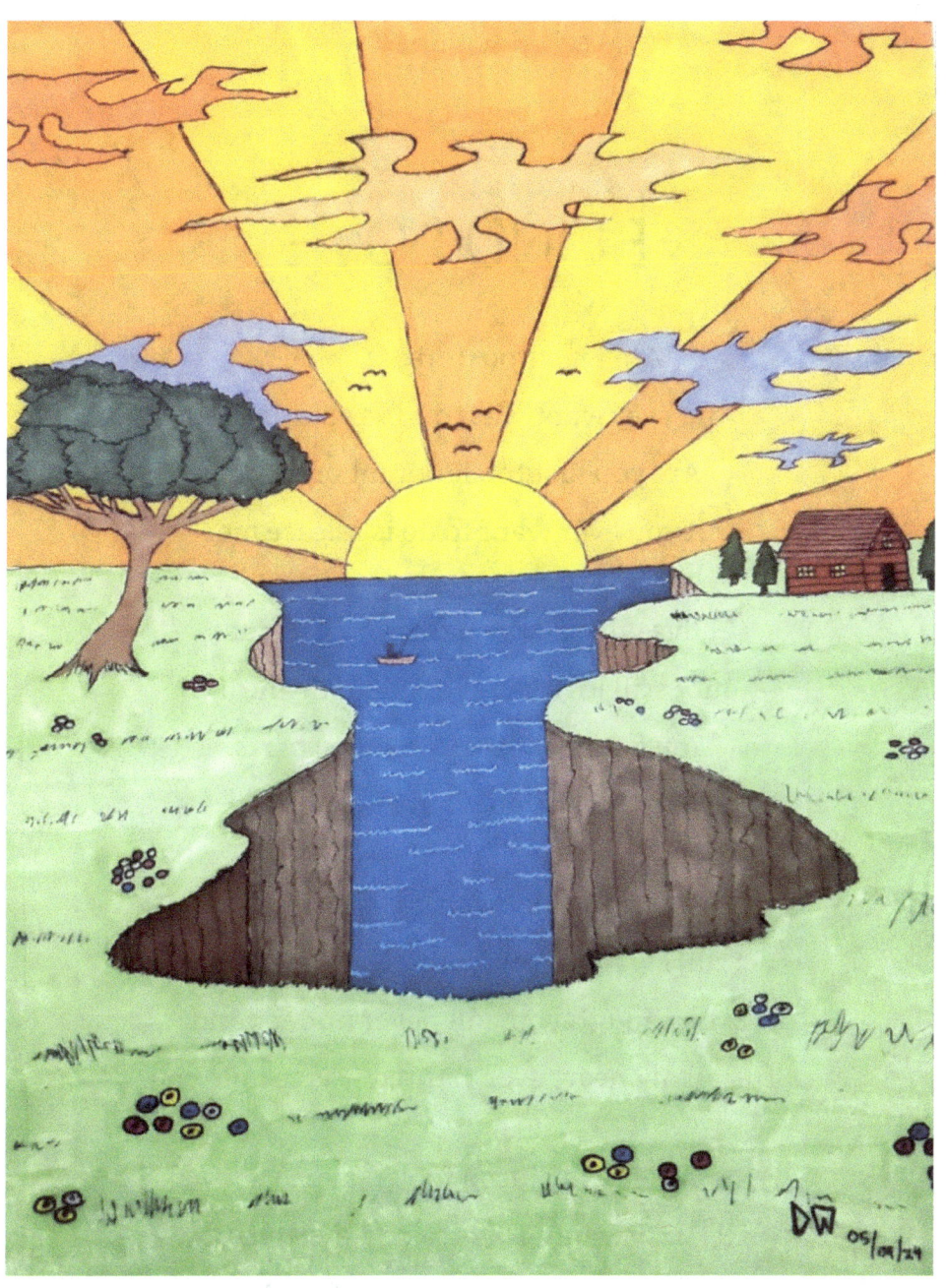

BLIND LOVE

Am I just too unreasonable?
All I ever want was to have your heart.
Are you just too ignorant of that?
All you ever want to do is release me.

I live with all the pains you give me.
But I still love you with all of my heart.
You cut my heart into many parts.
Still, I wish you would never hurt.

You make all my tears like no one.
Still, I want to put your pieces together.
Even though you will never understand.
Still, all my heart ever wanted was to love you.

Am I really just a fool in at heart?
All I ever wanted was to make you happy.
Are you really just heartless?
All you ever wanted was to not to think of me.

"PIECES"

May 18, 2024

Shattered and scattered, the fragments in this work speak to the universal experience of breaking and the relentless human drive to rebuild. Each piece is distinct—a shard of vibrant green, a fragment of bruised purple, a sliver of bold crimson—all seemingly unrelated yet harmoniously coming together to form something greater.

The textures within the fragments are rich with detail: jagged edges that tell of pain, smooth surfaces that hint at healing, and intricate patterns that carry whispers of memory. This is not a depiction of despair; it is a celebration of resilience. The work captures the quiet triumph of putting oneself back together, not as before, but as something stronger, more beautiful, and infinitely more whole.

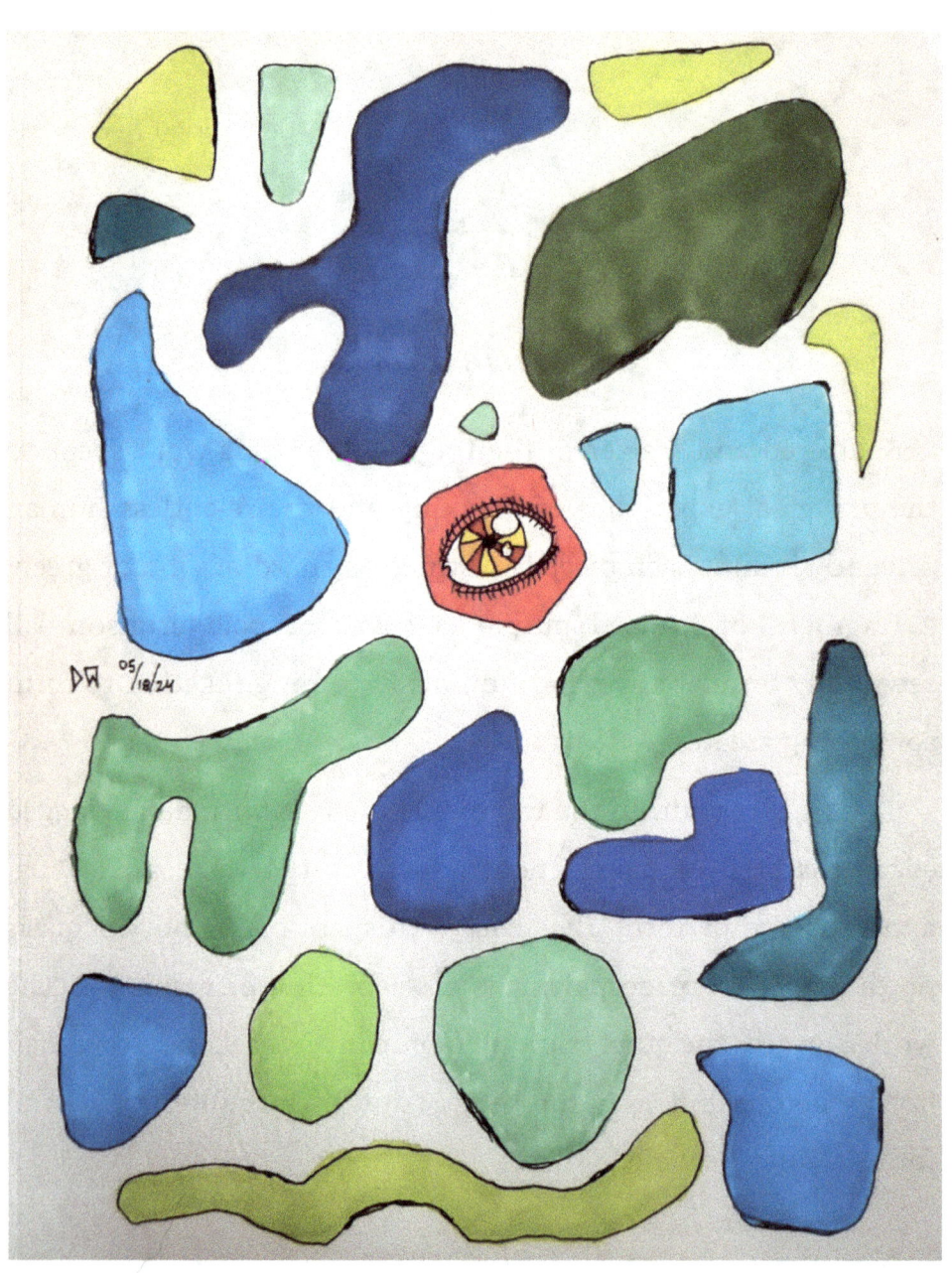

DROWNING IN DEADLINES

I feel as if though I am drowning in

Deadlines

&

Promises.

My red eyes, raw and weary, never rest.

I am burdened by the weight of

Time

&

Commitment.

My determination is slipping from my grasp.

Does my youth excuse my mistakes?

Surrounded by voices whispering all day and night.

Telling me, I have never made them proud.

Suffocating in the silent, unspoken disappointment in their eyes.

It's depressing, don't you think?

These feelings of anger and hurt are astounding.

Washing over me in overwhelming relentless tides.
The pain locking me in with a paralyzing ache.

I feel as if though I am drowning in
Deadlines
&
Promises.
The work, endless, pulls me deeper.

I wander through the darkness,
Seeking, hoping – yet unsure what for.
Perhaps a moment of peace, or a glimpse of pride,
A reminder that midst this chaos, I'm alive.

"TIME CRUNCH"

August 20, 2024

A vivid collision of color and movement, this piece captures the chaos of life under pressure. Spiraling clocks, fragmented gears, and darting arrows create a frenetic rhythm, symbolizing the relentless pull of deadlines. Bold yellows and reds exude urgency, while softer blues and greens offer fleeting moments of calm.

The dangling key hints at control or escape, a beacon amid the storm of obligations. Dynamic and unbalanced, *Time Crunch* embodies the tension of navigating time's unyielding pace, resonating with those who strive to find order within the chaos.

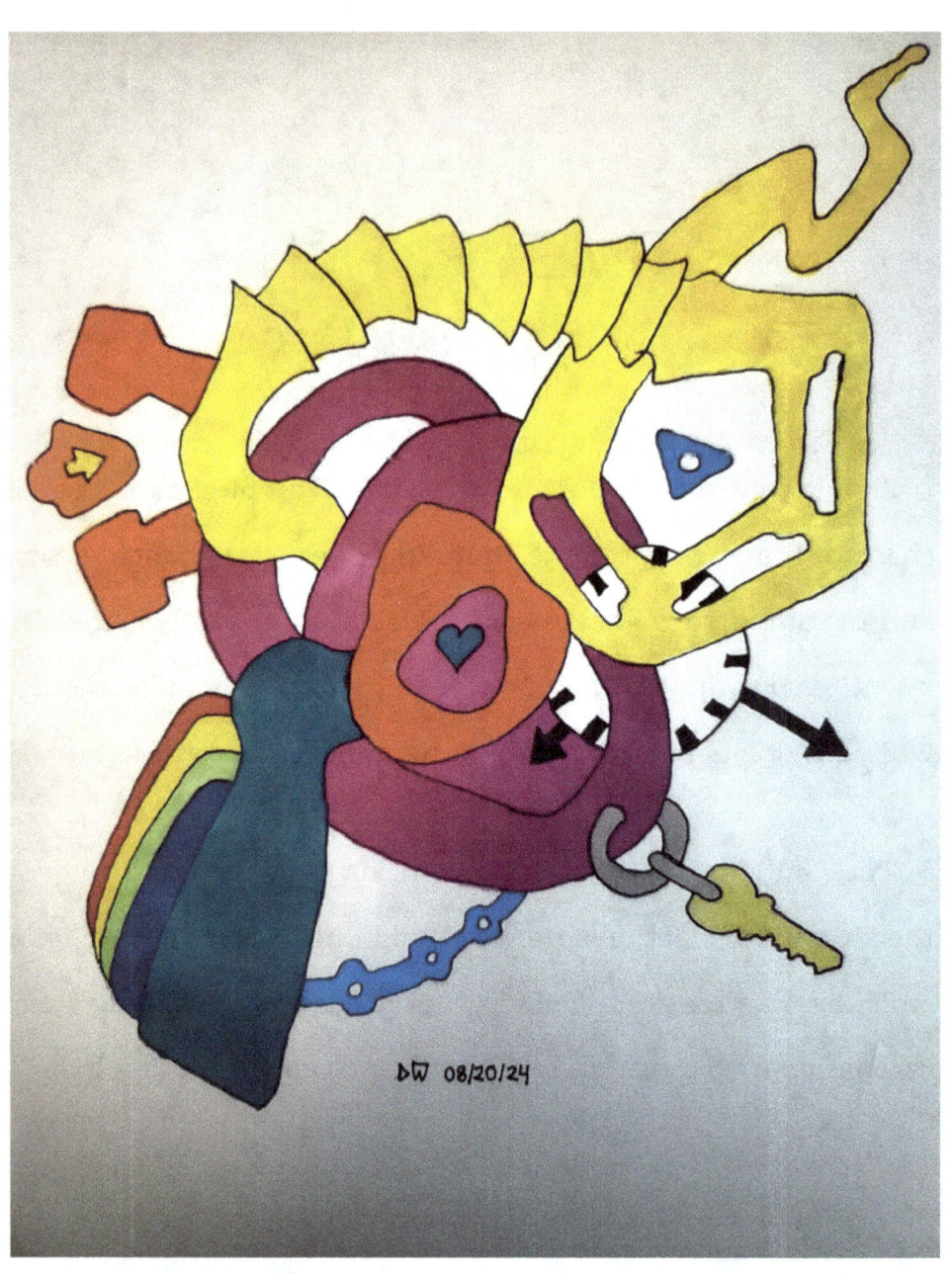

LOTUS

There is an emptiness that grows within me,
A loneliness no one else can see.
It eats at me slowly, this wicked feeling inside,
Coldness courses through my soul, felt from the outside.

What horrors await my broken, damaged heart?
Another glimpse of you—the man who tore it apart.
A void consumes me, devouring me whole,
Day by day, it threatens to swallow my tender soul.

Tell me, why did you just walk away?
Were your feelings so worthless, left to decay?
What happened to the words you once spoke with such care?
Was our cherished love nothing but air?

Are those treasured emotions now lost in time?
Was our love story to you merely a crime?
Can you not see the damage through the thickening smoke?
Or were my feelings for you just a cruel joke?

So, tell me, what am I to you?
A stranger, a friend, or a mistake you can't undo.
Why do your lips remain silent?
You gave my heart beatings so violently.

Tainted my soul with despair.
Left me with no hope to repair,
And now I wear a fake smile for the world to embrace.
But when I'm alone, I return to my darkest place.

This pain courses through me, so deep and malign,
Like a malignant cancer, it grows with no end in time.
How much more can my shattered heart endure?
How much further must it ache, so unsure?

I fear I am losing the will to keep living,
This void in my heart feeds on the pain you keep giving.
With every memory of us that drifts through my mind,
This void only grows, and I ask God why.

Death no longer scares me; I have no fear.
This void cuts silently, a blade slicing clear.
It engulfs me slowly, a disease borne of evil.
I am no angel, but you—you're no saint, either.

"LOTUS"

November 5, 2024

Emerging from a murky depth, the lotus in this illustration is a testament to beauty born of adversity. Its petals unfold in delicate layers, each one a soft gradient of white tinged with pink, glowing against the dark, chaotic background. The contrast between the serene flower and its harsh environment is striking, emphasizing the resilience required to bloom despite the odds.

The water below is depicted with a turbulent texture, rippling with the echoes of unseen struggles. Yet the lotus rises undeterred, its stem a beacon of quiet strength. This is a piece that speaks not only to survival but to the triumph of thriving, reminding viewers that from the darkest places, the most profound beauty can emerge.

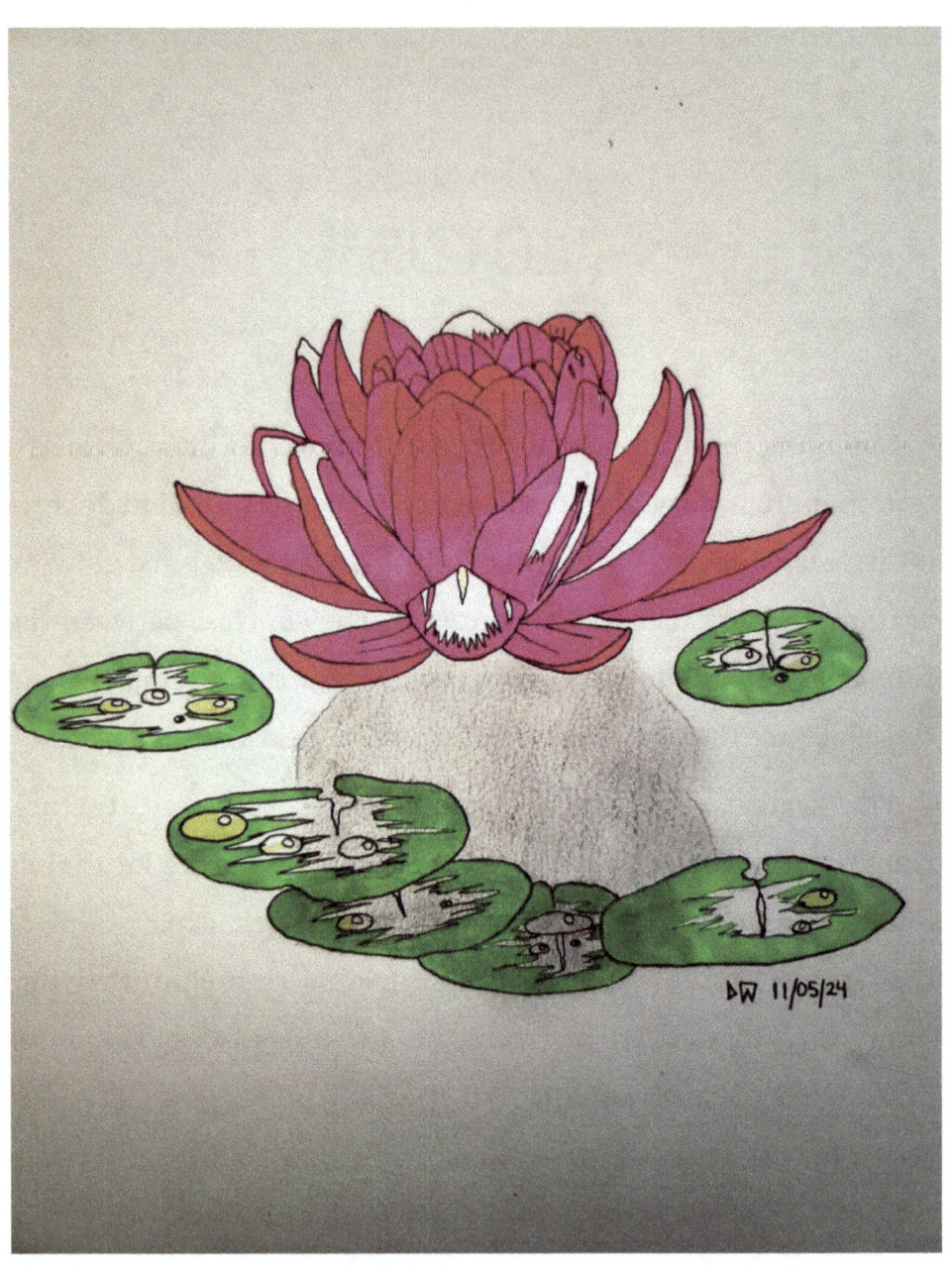

I AM YOUR DISEASE

You know who I am.
You've called me your friend.
Wishes of misery and heartache, I send.
I want only to see brought to your knees.
I am the devil inside you,
I am your disease.

I'll invade all your thoughts.
I'll take hostage of your soul.
I'll become your new master.
I'll have total control.
I'll maim your emotions.
I'll run the whole game,
'Till your entire existence is crippled with shame.

When you call me,
Sometimes I come in disguise.
Quite often, I take you by surprise.
And take you, I will.

Just as you feared.

I only want to hurt you, with no mercy spared.

As for your family, I'll see its destruction.

I'll steal every pleasure in your life you ever enjoyed.

I'll not only hurt you, but I'll also kill if I please.

I'm your worst living nightmare.

I am your disease.

I bring ways of self-destruction.

Can't you tell?

I'll sweep you through Heaven, then drop you into Hell.

Don't you see,

I'll choose you forever.

Wherever you go, I'll catch you.

You won't see it coming, you won't even know.

Sometimes, I lay silent,

Waiting for the strike.

What was once yours will become mine.

I take what I like.

I'll take all you own.

I don't care who sees.

I am your constant companion.

I am your disease.

If you have any honor,

I'll strip it away.

You will lose all your hope.

You'll forget how to pray and become blind.

I will leave you in the darkness.

I'll reduce you to nothing.

I don't care.

Don't underestimate my powers.

I'll bend you until you break,

Time after time.

I'll make the world that surrounds you crumble,

With great ease.

Can't you see?

I'm that mad person you hide inside you.

I am your disease.

But I must say, today, I am really angry.

You want to know why?

You seem not to care what I say, it's like you're not listening.

How did I lose my grip on you?

Where did I go wrong?

Have you gone deaf?

One minute I had you, the next its like you were gone.

Listen to me!
You can't dismiss all the good times we've shared.
When you were alone,
Wasn't it I who was there for you?
When you sold your possessions,
Wasn't it I who supported and urged you to do so.
I knew what you needed.

Oh, how sad this is to me, to watch you ignore me.
You believe that you're thinking clear now.
That you've escaped me with your life.
You think you found the way out of this by
Seeking help from therapist, medications, family, and friends.
Oh, what fools they are for trying to help you.
They tell you; you've won the war with me when you
admitted defeat in the battles and sought help.

Okay, go ahead and surrender,
If that's what you choose.
I'm not giving up.
I can't stand to lose.
I will not be damned into failure.

Be damned all your therapy,

Be damned all your AA meetings,
Be damned you Higher Power, however unique.
Be damned all your prayers.
Be damned every addict,
Back to me they eventually stray.

I know it will happen,
I've witnessed it many times before.
Those who love misery, always come back crawling for more.
So, you better take comfort in knowing,
I'll be by your side, always, waiting for the
next time you come around.
I am your disease.

You feel like you're stronger and smarter this time,
Feel as if though there isn't a mountain you can't climb.
Well, if you believe that, you haven't learned a thing.
I'll still come knocking,
Waiting for the day you step back into my ring.

But you say you are done with me,
So, what can I do?
It is sad in a way,
I had big plans for you.
Creating your nightmare was a dream to me.

I'm going to miss you,

We made quite a team.

Don't forget me,

I won't forget you.

I promise I will always stand by your side,

Watching all that you do.

I'll be waiting and ready.

Call whenever you please.

I'm close by, inside you.

I am your disease.

"SELF-GROWTH"

September 15, 2024

This intricate piece portrays growth as a dynamic and chaotic process. Twisting forms spiral upward, their lines both jagged and fluid, suggesting struggle and perseverance. The bold colors—deep greens, fiery oranges, and radiant yellows—pulse with vitality, reflecting the energy required to break through barriers and reach for the light.

The background is textured with shadowy undertones, grounding the piece in the reality that growth often emerges from pain and uncertainty. Yet the overall composition is one of optimism, as the upward movement dominates, carrying with it the promise of transformation. It is a celebration of the messy, beautiful journey toward becoming.

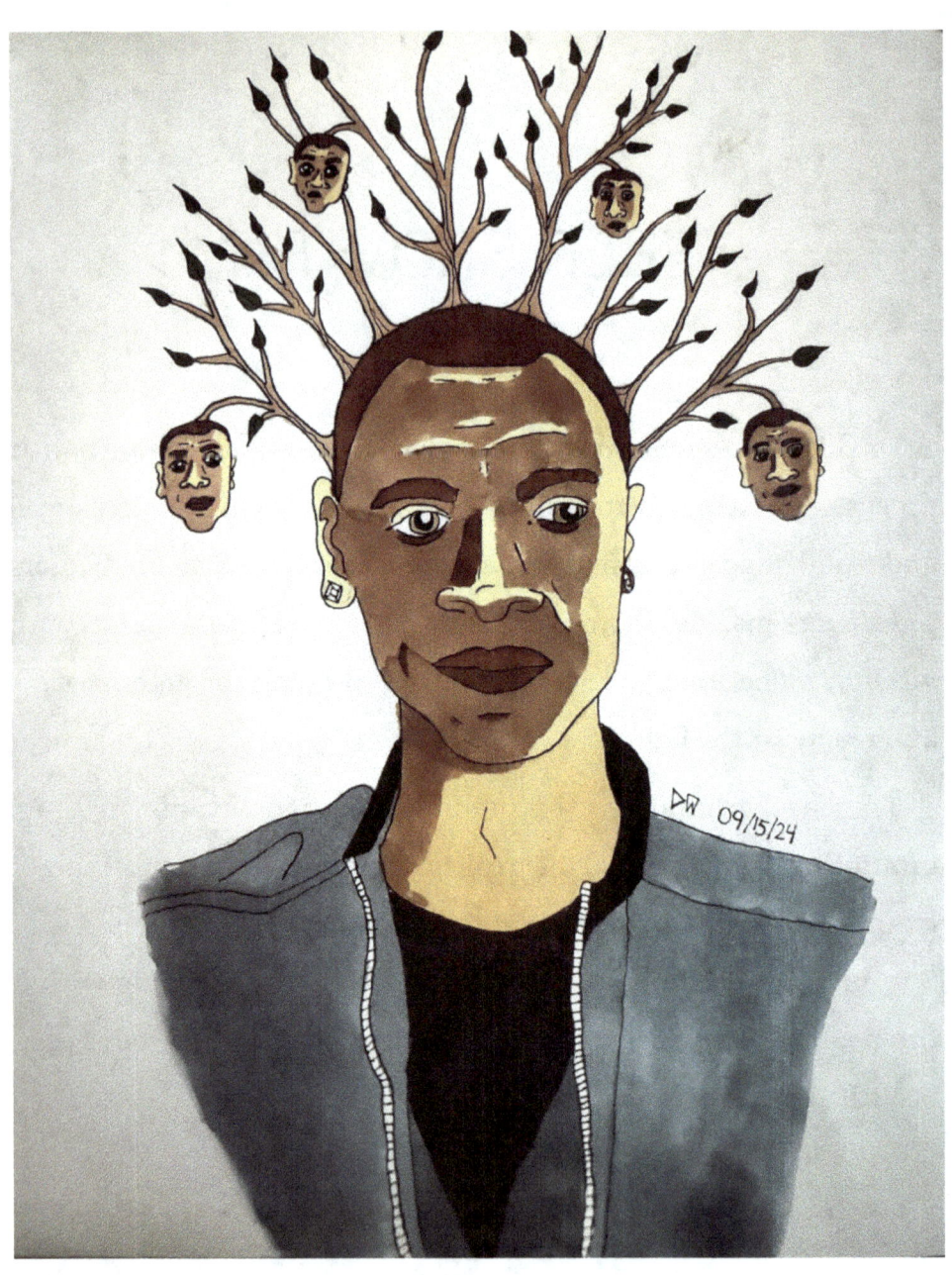

LOVE UNVEILED

I never told you how I truly feel.
Being with you feels so surreal.
Love is our connection.
It will give our lives a meaningful direction.

With our love combined everything is in our reach.
Together we can stand any siege.
Words cannot express how you have
captured my heart with success.

Our life together has just begun.
We fit together like moon and sun.
I anxiously await our time ahead.
With impatience, I am fed.

All of you is what I need.
Together, we will succeed.
I look forward to our next moment together
Without you, my pain cannot be measured.

"STOP & GO"

August 24, 2024

This striking piece transforms an everyday traffic signal into a bold exploration of decision-making and life's rhythm. The vibrant reds, yellows, and greens command attention, while the deep, layered background of purples and oranges evokes the fleeting beauty of a sunset, adding emotional depth to the mundane.

The structured geometry of the signal contrasts with the organic flow of the colors around it, creating tension between control and freedom. The artwork captures the pauses, hesitations, and movements that shape our journeys, celebrating the interplay between action and reflection in the ever-changing flow of life.

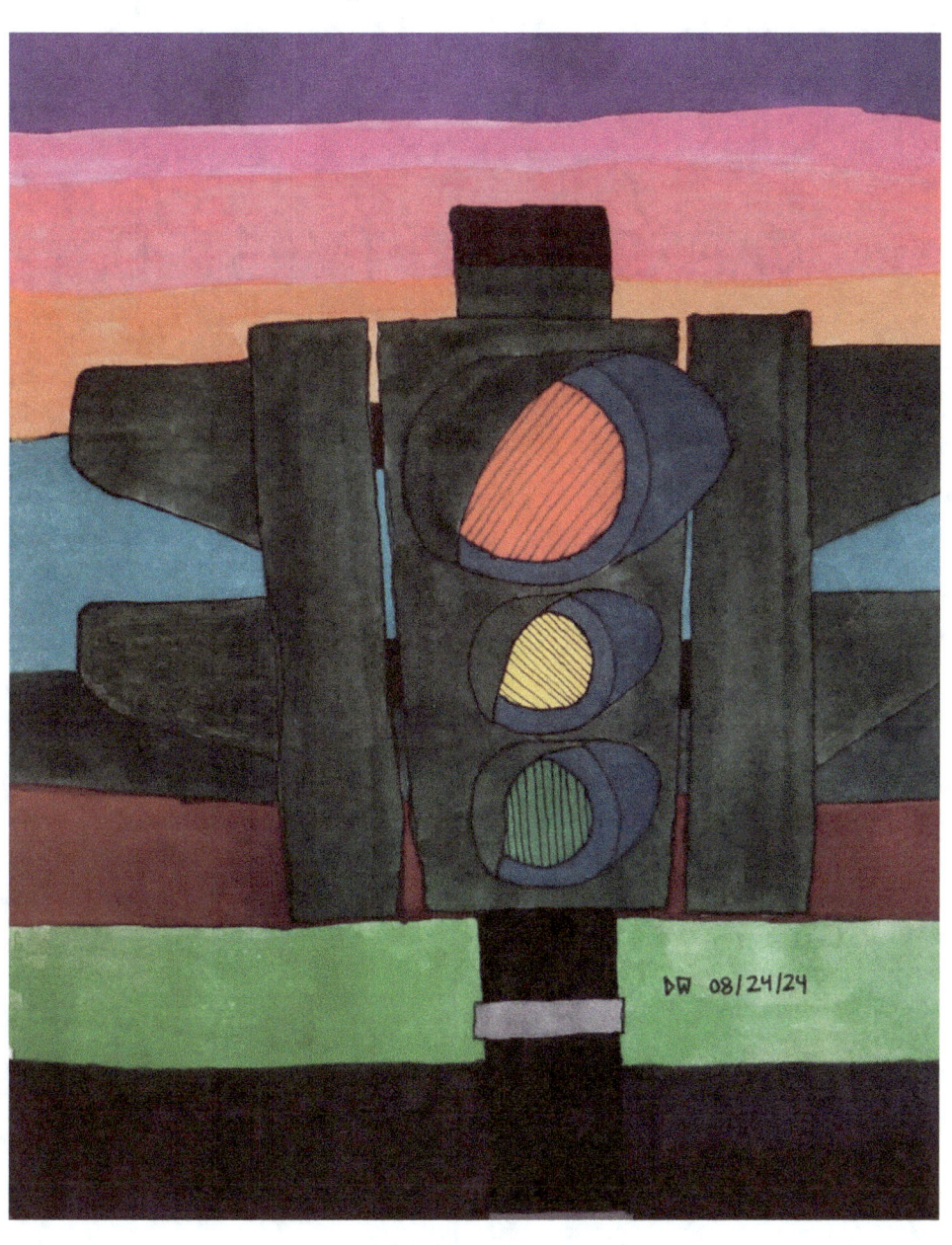

WARPED AND TWISTED

Harsh words and violent blows.
Hidden secrets nobody knows.
Eyes are open, hands are fisted.
Deep inside I'm warped and twisted.

So many tricks and so many lies.
Too many when's and too many whys.
Nobody is special, nobody is gifted.
I'm just me, warped and twisted.

Sleeping awake and chocking on a dream.
Listening loudly to a silent scream.
Call my mind, the number isn't listed.
Lost in someone, so warped and twisted.

On my knees, alive but dead.
Look at the invisible blood I have bled.
I'm not gone, my mind has drifted.
Don't expect much, I'm warped and twisted.

Burnt out, wasted, and hollow.
Today is just yesterday's tomorrow.
The sun died out; the ashes sifted.
I'm still here warped and twisted.

"FACEFEAR"

May 19, 2024

A raw and unyielding portrayal of the battle against inner demons, this piece is alive with intensity. Stark contrasts of black and white dominate the composition, while jagged streaks of fiery red cut through the darkness like wounds left exposed. The central figure, partially obscured and fragmented, seems to reach outward and inward simultaneously, grappling with something unseen but deeply felt.

The chaotic strokes that surround the figure mimic the sensation of spiraling thoughts and relentless fear, yet there is a steadiness in the figure's core. This is not a scene of surrender but of defiance, capturing the moment when fear is met with unwavering resolve.

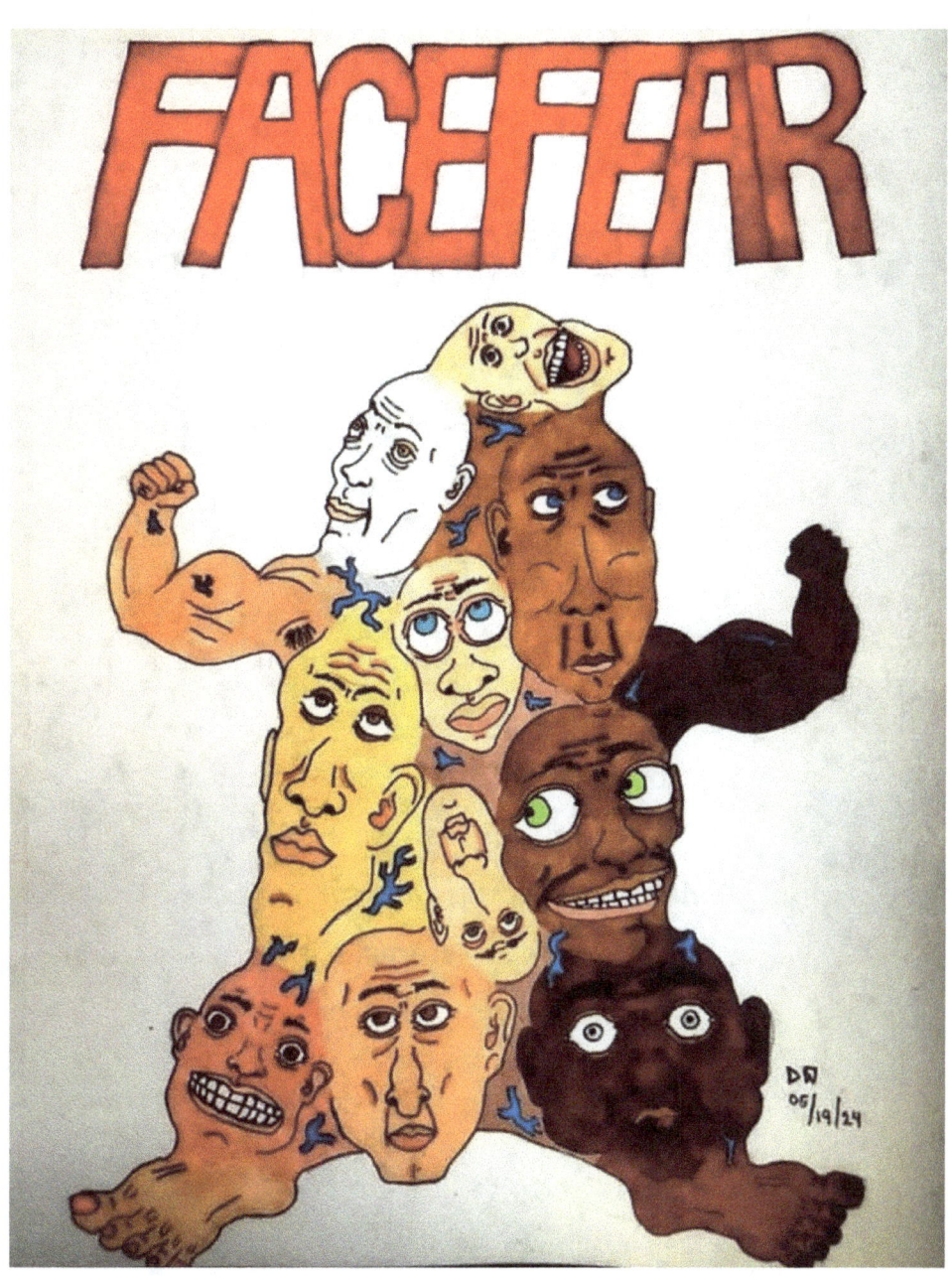

IF FATE WERE KINDER

If fate were kinder,

By now, we would be holding hands.

In each other's arms.

staring on both eyes,

Locking lips,

And laughing to the contentment of our hearts.

If fate were kinder,

We would have dreamt of our dreams.

And loved fully.

Feel that deep ecstasy and surrender.

Be drowned by eternal bliss.

If fate were just kinder.

"PSYCHEDELIC SUNFLOWER"

August 18, 2024

Bursting with radiant energy, this sunflower transcends its natural form to become a mesmerizing kaleidoscope of colors and patterns. The vibrant yellow petals extend outward like rays of sunlight, while the intricate, multicolored mandala at its core pulses with dynamic intensity. This fusion of organic beauty and abstract design brings a surreal, dreamlike quality to the piece.

The lush green leaves and stem anchor the sunflower in reality, but the hypnotic patterns at the center draw viewers into a world of boundless imagination.

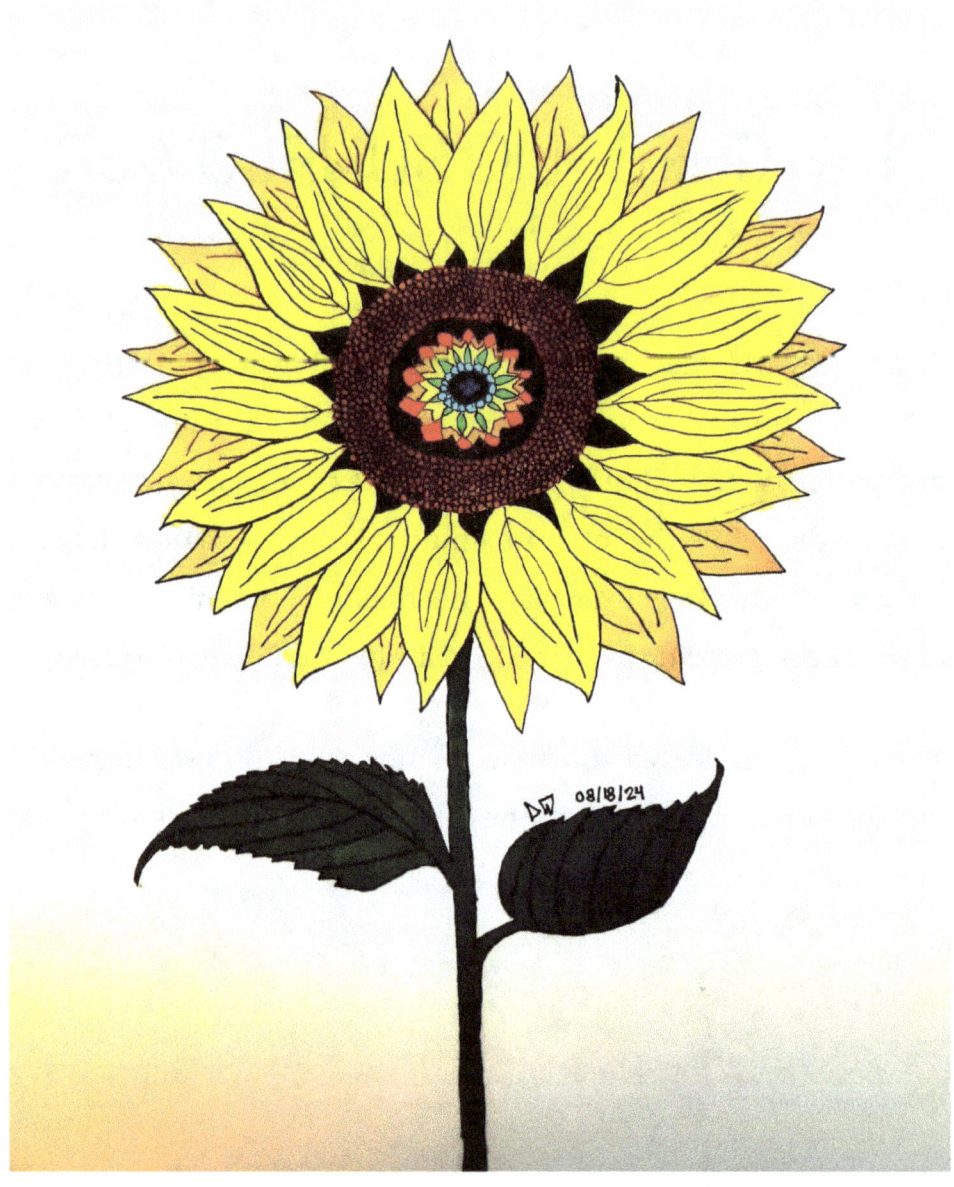

BLACK ROSE

Beautiful and unique
But also, quite terrifying
Alone in a bed of colorful flowers
Always left unwanted.

Beautiful black rose
Alone and thorny
Different and feared
None appreciates its beauty.

Many wanted to pick it
But no one dared to reach it
The only one left among its peers
A new generation now surrounds it.

I've watched it for quite some time
It is as lonely as me
I picked it up and carried it back home
Decided it to plant it in a pot

I will take care of this rose

So, we'll no longer be alone

I will appreciate your uniqueness

Because we are as lonely as each other.

"BLACK ROSE"

December 1, 2024

A striking symbol of mystery and resilience, this piece draws the eye with its bold contrasts and emotional depth. The black rose, with its velvety petals, rises against a vivid crimson diamond background, exuding both elegance and defiance. The deep green leaves and stem provide a grounding balance to the intensity of the rose itself, emphasizing its unique beauty.

The juxtaposition of dark and vibrant colors captures the complex duality of the rose—its capacity to symbolize both strength and solitude, beauty and melancholy. *Black Rose* serves as a poignant reminder of individuality and the quiet power of thriving against all odds.

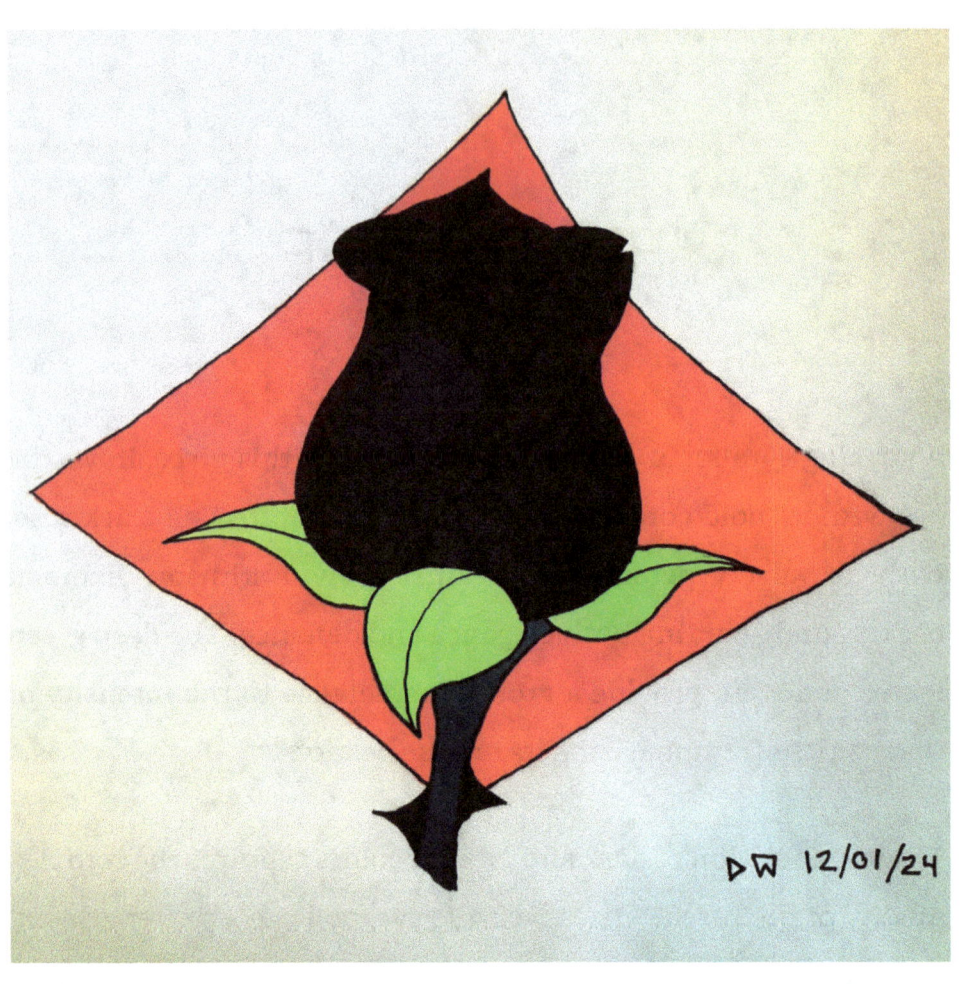

LOVING YOU, LOSING ME

Loving you felt like shoes on the wrong feet,
Every step is unsteady, an incomplete beat.
I could still move, but something felt wrong,
A rhythm off-key in a broken song.

Loving you felt like the wrong side of the bed,
Each morning heavy, a fog in my head.
The sun would rise, but I couldn't see,
The weight of frustration consuming me.

Loving you felt like living alone,
Sharing space, yet my heart turned to stone.
Hours of silence, a ghost by my side,
Your presence forgotten; my loneliness amplified.

Loving you felt like pouring too deep,
Draining my soul, no strength left to keep.
I gave you my all, down to the last drop,
Yet the cup stayed empty, and I couldn't stop.

Loving you felt like gasping for air,
Anxiety gripping, a breathless despair.
My lungs collapsed under love's cruel sting,
An endless fall without a wing.

Loving you felt like signing my death,
I'd give my last heartbeat, my final breath.
Like Juliet longing for Romeo's embrace,
I would have died to be loved in your space.

"CRUISING"

September 7, 2024

A bold and electrifying vision of freedom and defiance, this piece captures the thrill of traversing a surreal, untamed landscape. The lone biker, clad in crimson armor, exudes power and mystery as they navigate a winding road lined with otherworldly phenomena. Flames dance in vibrant orange and blue, defying gravity, while crystalline formations shimmer under an alien sky streaked with deep greens and blues.

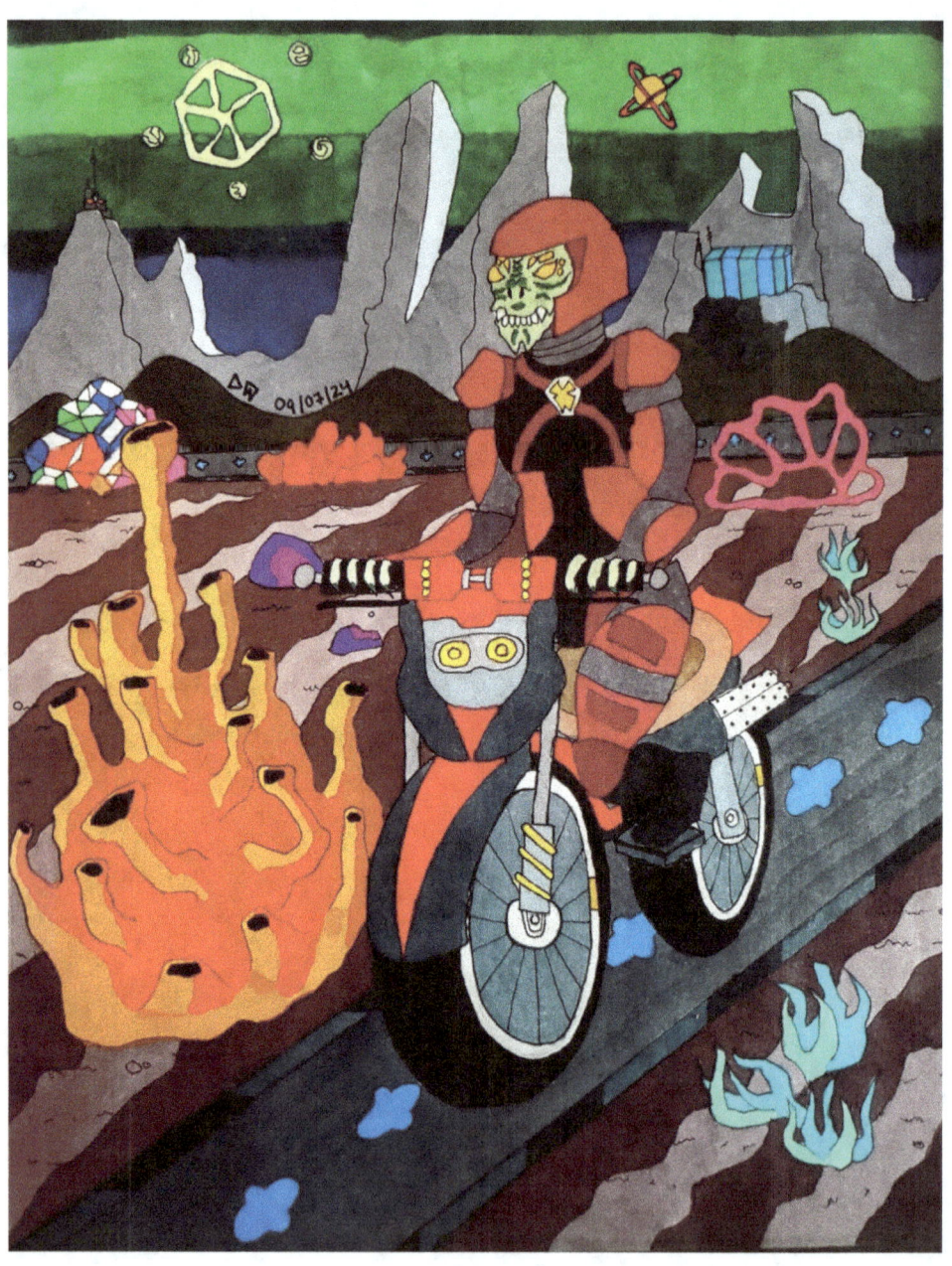

RACE

My life became a race to outrun the voices,
They claimed I had made all the wrong choices.
"You're not good enough," they whispered with glee,
Their words hit hard, cutting deep into me.

They told me I ran but got nowhere at all,
Stealing my breath, making me feel small.
"You'll never succeed," they drilled in my mind,
These voices were cruel, unrelenting, unkind.

Inside and out, they followed my trail,
Haunting each moment, ensuring I'd fail.
No matter how fast my feet struck the ground,
Their taunting words always found me around.

"Don't cheer them on," I begged through my tears,
Their sneers grew louder, feeding my fears.
So, I tried to escape in bottles of beer,
But their cruel jeers only became more clear.

At night, I wondered, do tears feel pain,
When they fall and shatter like drops of rain?
"Don't feed the gremlins," I silently pled,
"They'll bite and leave scars that you'll never shed."

Their voices were sharp, a piercing refrain,
"You're worthless, a failure—wallow in shame."
I drowned in their venom, my gown pulling me deep,
In my mind's dark ocean, I sank to weep.

Their game was my pain, a relentless spree,
Illogical torment that blinded me.
"Useless, disgusting, a waste of space,"
Their cruel echoes filled every place.

But then you came, with a light so warm,
Taming the storm and calming the swarm.
You silenced the chaos that rattled my head,
And gave me hope where I saw only dread.

It took every ounce of me not to kiss you,
As my mind battled and the gremlins bit through.
But your presence gave me the strength to fight,
To reclaim my power and find the light.

With you, the voices began to fade,
Their power shattered; their torment stayed.
Your laughter healed what they defiled,
And for the first time, I truly smiled.

You kissed my soul and woke me anew,
Like crisp leaves falling, the world felt true.
The voices retreated, their lies untold,
Their venom turned to fine-spun gold.

In your gaze, I saw my worth revealed,
The wounds they left began to heal.
With every whisper, every glance,
You gave me courage, a second chance.

Now I stand, no longer afraid,
You love my shelter, my barricade.
Together, we've built a fortress strong,
In your arms, I know I belong.

No longer running, I've found my way,
With you, my love, I choose to stay.
Hand in hand, we'll face the fight,
With you, everything feels right.

Through every valley and mountain steep,
With you beside me, my heart will keep.
For you are the dream I've long pursued,
In your love, my spirit renewed.

Here's to the future, bright and clear,
A love that deepens year after year.
With every breath, every embrace,
I've found my home, my sacred space.

No longer bound by the voices' reign,
With you, I'm free—free from the pain.
Together, we'll write this endless song,
With you, my love, I've found where I belong.

"DEMOLITION"

September 7, 2024

A chaotic race through an electrifying universe, this piece brims with motion and energy, depicting an otherworldly demolition derby on intergalactic highways. A flamboyant orange creature, clad in futuristic gear, speeds across a winding golden track in a retro-style vehicle, exuding confidence and thrill. The vibrant colors and exaggerated details create a sense of surrealism, with twisting roads defying gravity and vehicles tearing through the fabric of space. The background bursts with layers of emerald green skies, deep indigo depths, and a glowing red planet, setting the stage for the cosmic chaos.

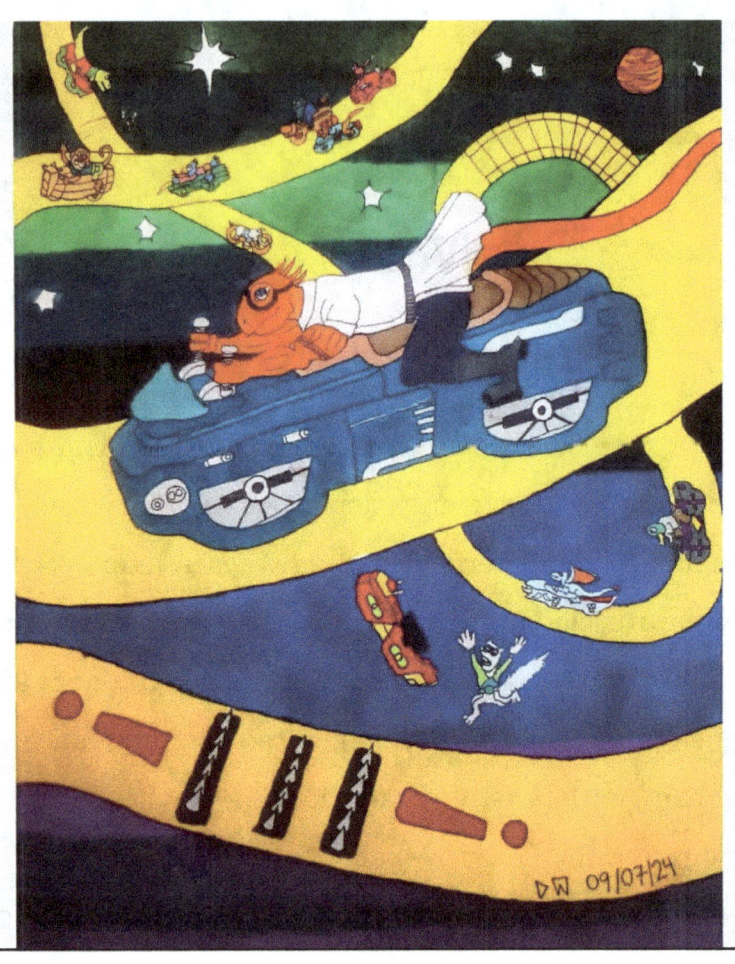

INVISIBLE THREAD

I think when two souls fall in love, you'll see,
It's written in their eyes, as clear as can be.
The way they glance, the way they stare,
A silent confession lingering there.

Their gaze is filled with admiration and need,
A fire that burns, a love guaranteed.
Eyes that twinkle with unspoken desire,
A spark ignited, a consuming fire.

And matched with their smiles, so full of grace,
Hope and happiness light up their faces.
It's funny how, without words being said,
We all can see that invisible thread.

A bond unseen, yet forever entwined,
Two hearts connected; one fate aligned.
No distance or time could sever the line,
For love like theirs is purely divine.

"FANTASY NIGHTSCAPE"

June 8, 2024

A majestic unicorn wades through shimmering waters under a glowing crescent moon. Its flowing rainbow mane illuminates the dark, star-streaked sky, while vibrant green hills and fiery cliffs frame the scene with surreal beauty. The rich colors and serene composition blend myth and magic, creating a dreamlike world that sparks wonder and imagination. *Fantasy Nightscape* captures the timeless allure of the fantastical, inviting viewers to lose themselves in its enchanting glow.

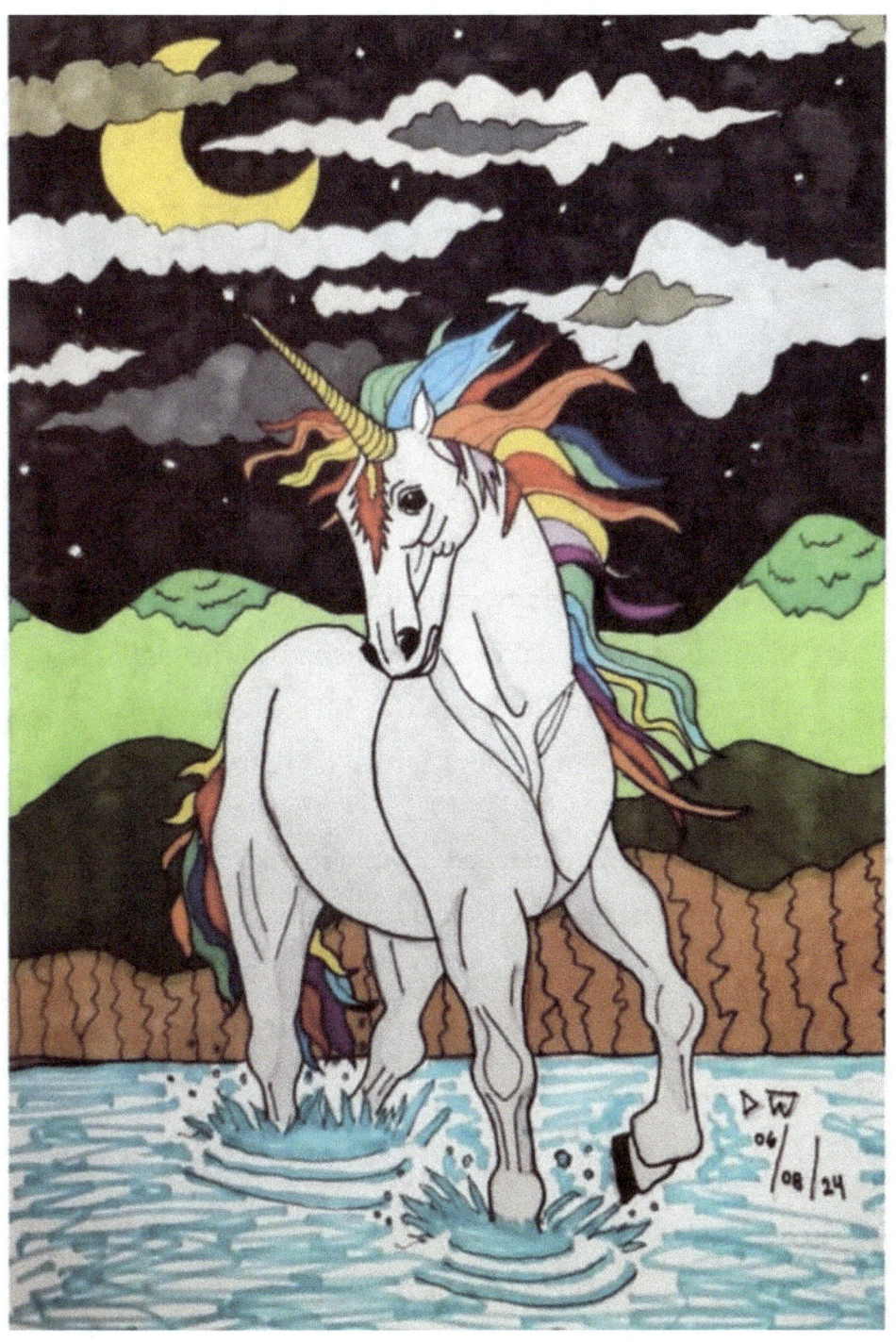

LOVE'S TRUE MUSE

I stopped writing for a little while,
The reasons unclear, no cause, no trial.
I'd always used my poetry to heal,
To mend my wings and help me feel.

Then one day, you came into view,
Through ups and downs, we pushed on through.
Day by day, your love did grow,
Replacing my frowns with a radiant glow.

My pen untouched, my notebook still,
Yet my heart found words that time can't kill.
I realized then, as clear as can be,
When I speak to you, my speech is poetry.

No paper needed, no ink to flow,
For love writes verses the heart will show.
You've become the muse that sets me free,
My every word, now poetry.

"THE ALL KNOWING"

August 17, 2024

Geometric precision meets vivid abstraction in this striking depiction of wisdom and omniscience. The face, composed of angular shapes in shades of purple, red, and blue, exudes an aura of calm authority. Piercing yellow eyes anchor the piece, drawing the viewer into its depths, while a subtle rainbow prism at the forehead suggests enlightenment and infinite awareness.

The symmetry of the composition evokes balance and clarity, while the vibrant color palette adds an element of mystique. *The All Knowing* captures the essence of insight and understanding, inviting viewers to reflect on the boundless nature of knowledge and the mysteries it holds.

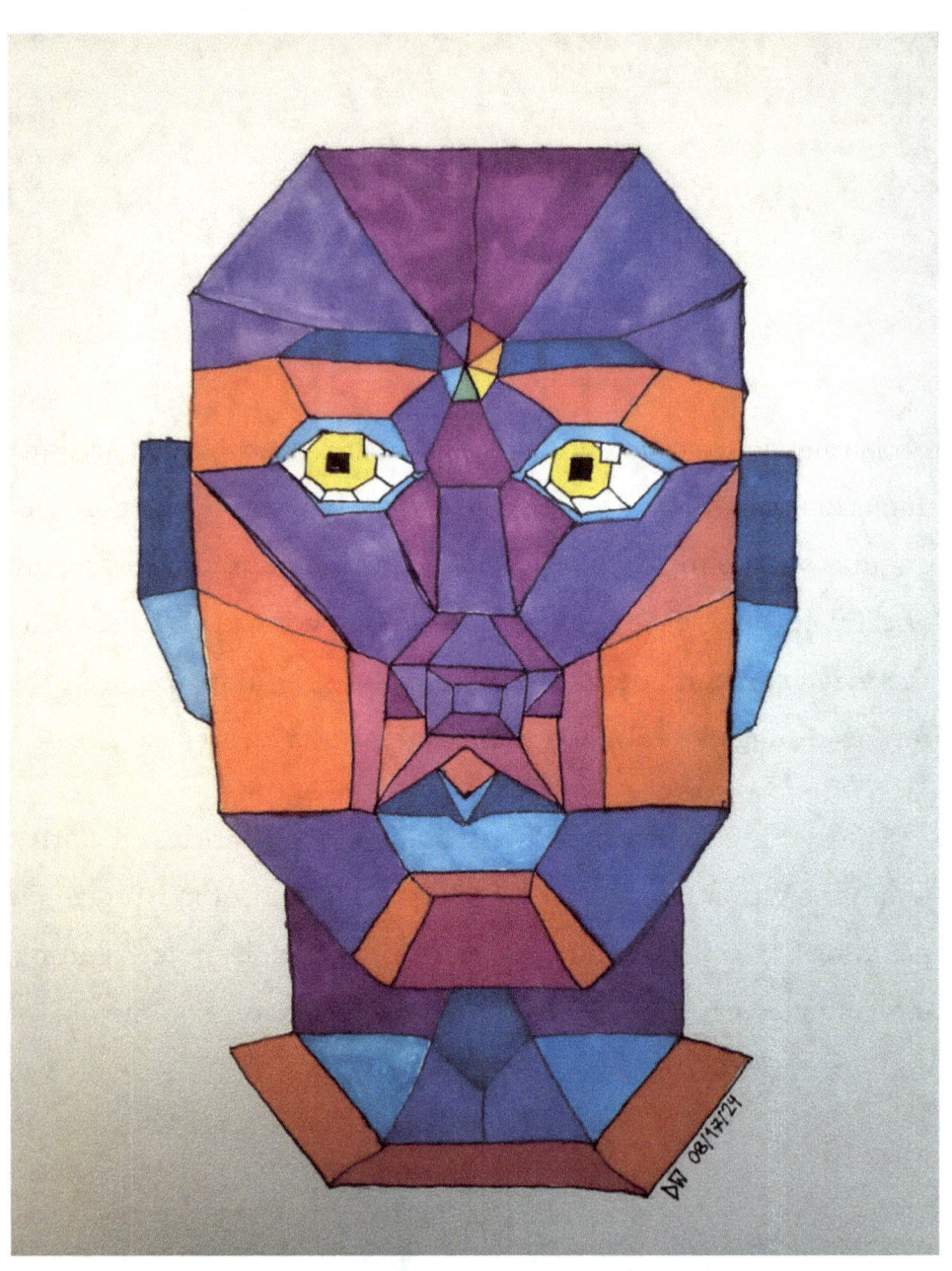

BROKEN PROMISE

She's only eighteen, her life just begun,
But the weight of the world feels like it weighs a ton.
She hates school, where they laugh and stare,
Every cruel word makes her question who's there.

Her sister says, "This isn't how it seems,
There's hope in the night, and light in your dreams."
But each day she sinks further, drowning in despair,
She hides the pain, but her scars are laid bare.

She tried to leave it all with a handful of pills,
Hoping to silence the chaos, the thrills.
Sitting by her bed, she feels numb inside,
Her sister reaches out, but the pain won't subside.

She holds her close, but the resistance persists,
Until her eyes find the scars on her wrists.
"Why do you do this? Why choose this pain?
Tell me, dear sister, what do you gain?"

She whispers, "It's control; the pain's mine to decide.
It's the only way I can calm the storm inside."
Her sister pleads, tears falling like rain,
"How long has this been your escape from the pain?"

"It's been a while; I just needed some luck."
Her sister screams, "Promise me, baby, never cut!
No one may get you, you might feel alone,
But I'm here to remind you, you're never on your own."

"So, baby, don't cut, baby, don't cut,
You're stronger than this—just promise you'll trust.
I know the blade feels like your only friend,
But, baby, don't cut—this isn't the end."

The next day at school, she felt light on her feet,
Even smiled as she walked through the crowded street.
But laughter erupted when her books hit the floor,
And the whispers and stares returned once more.

She couldn't take it, so she sent her sister a text,
"I love you to death, in this life and the next."
Her sister didn't know what it meant,
She texted back feverishly until her heart was spent.

Skipping her class, she ran home to her room,
Thinking, "I won't break my promise this soon."
But one cut… two cuts… three cuts… four,
Blood spilled silently onto the floor.

Her sister felt dread rise in her chest,
A fear she couldn't shake, a weight she couldn't rest.
She raced home, bursting through the door,
Called out her sister's name as she checked every floor.

She found her there by the bathtub's side,
Her tears and her blood flowing like a tide.
"Stay with me, baby!" She begged through her cries,
As she drifted away, she stared into her eyes.

Paramedics arrived, rushed her through the halls,
The doctor worked fast, fighting death's calls.
An hour passed, and the doctor returned,
With sorrow in his voice, his face stern.

"I'm sorry for your loss," he softly said,
Her sister collapsed as her world turned red.
Her guilt screamed loud, "How could I let this be?
Baby, you promised you'd never leave me!"

The pain remains, the scars stay etched,
A memory of the one she tried to protect.
It does not go away with time,
The words still lingered, haunting her mind.

"Baby, don't cut, baby, don't cut,
You're worth so much more than giving up.
Though the road feels dark and full of despair,
Know someone loves you—someone cares."

"302"

August 31, 2024

A tranquil blend of nostalgia and comfort, this piece invites viewers into the idyllic charm of a countryside home. The bright yellow house, framed by red accents and nestled against a backdrop of rolling green hills and snow-capped mountains, radiates warmth and familiarity. The scene is brought to life with meticulous details: a winding stone path leads to the front door, a vibrant red car rests in the driveway, and a sparkling pool glimmers under the golden sunlight.

The clear blue sky, dotted with fluffy white clouds, enhances the serenity of the setting, while the neatly manicured lawn and surrounding trees evoke a sense of timeless simplicity.

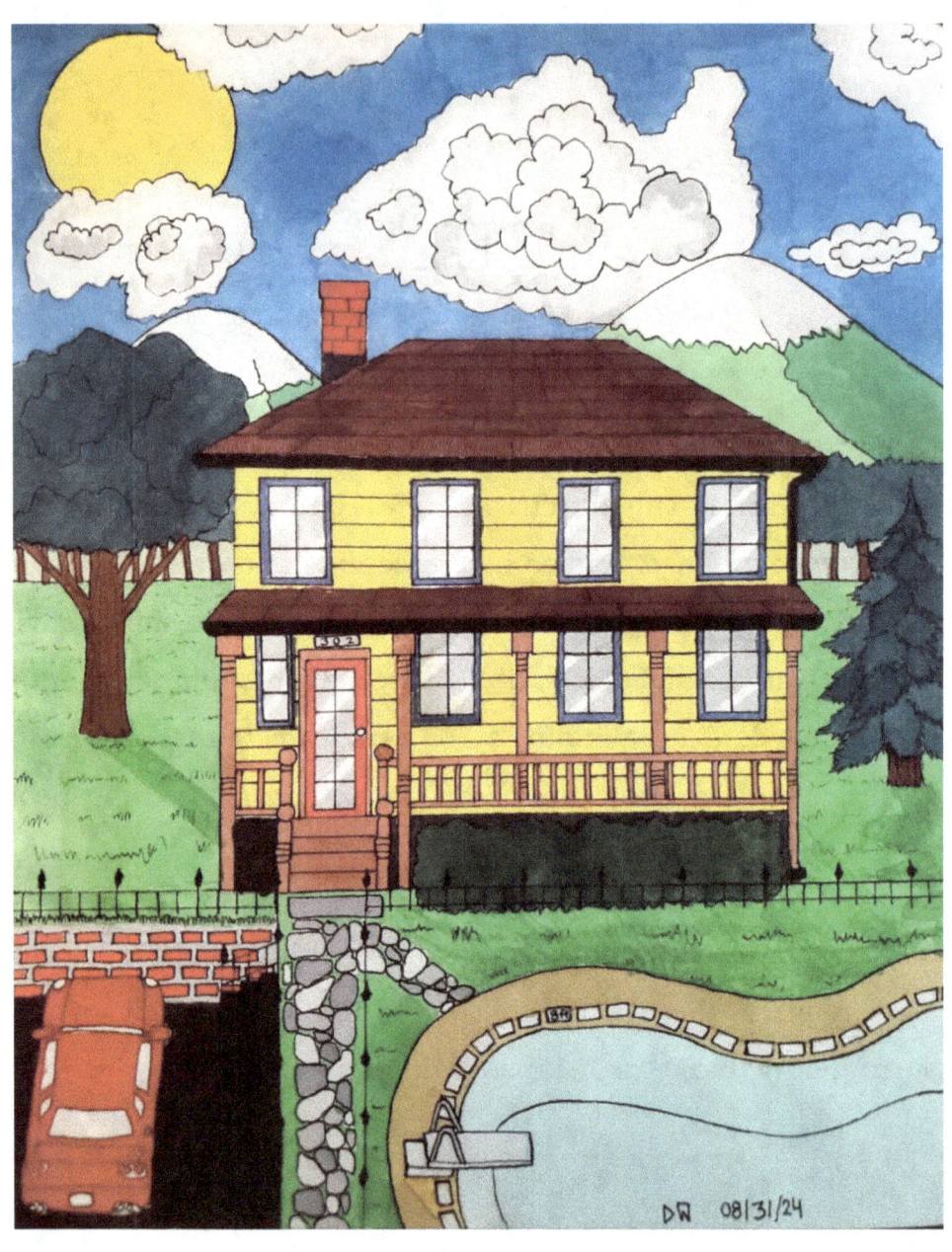

MY DOOR'S KEY

Depression is lying, a clever disguise,
It's me saying, "I'm fine," while my spirit dies.
Faking a laugh to cover the pain,
While tears fall silently, again and again.

I promise, this stillness is not from lack of trying,
But your words cut deep, their echoes denying:
"Happiness is a choice," "You'll be okay,"
"You've nothing to be sad about today."

No one would choose this endless fight,
This shadowed world with no guiding light.
For years I've battled this heavy despair,
Wishing for freedom, gasping for air.

You don't see the demons that whisper and jeer,
You can't hear their lies or feel the fear.
The weight they place, crushing inside,
It's hidden from view, so I learned to hide.

When did we decide to ignore the disease,
To take "I'm fine" at face value with ease?
When did we stop looking behind the mask,
Or hearing the truth in the questions we ask?

But maybe the problem isn't just you,
Maybe I've built walls too high to break through.
Perhaps it's my voice that's been denying,
Hiding the pain, pretending, and lying.

I've decided to speak, to tell what is real:
I'm hurting, I'm struggling, I can barely feel.
Sometimes I suffocate, gasping for air,
Wishing I'd let you in, but too full of despair.

Maybe it's not you, but me, holding the key,
The lock on my door that keeps you from me.
And if I could open, if I could let you see,
Maybe everything would change with my door's key.

On the worst days, depression is a fog,
A cloud so thick I'm lost in the smog.
It steals my thoughts, leaves me numb inside,
Trapping me where the shadows reside.

My room, once a haven, is now a cell,
Darker than any prisoner's hell.
I'm not alone, yet I'm never free,
For the demon inside has taken me.

Depression is possession, a cruel lie,
I'm just an object it claims as its prize.
Thoughts race and crash, relentless, unkind,
Leaving me blind to what's ahead, stuck behind.

Mistakes replay like a haunting refrain,
Every choice, every step, just leads to pain.
Regrets flow fast, like tears in the shower,
Hoping to cleanse, to regain my power.

But the water won't wash the shame away,
It clings to my soul, a price I must pay.

On the best days, I forget it exists,
The weight, the whispers, the clenched fists.
I'm not just surviving—I truly thrive,
Feeling alive, my soul revived.

On good days, my room's no longer a cage,
It's a sanctuary where I turn the page.

The demons retreat, the lies fade away,
And I feel the sun light my way.

Mental illness is there, a shadow I see,
But I've learned it is not my identity.
On those days, I remember who I can be,
A person with strength, resilient and free.

But fear of judgment-built walls around me,
A fortress I thought would protect and keep me.
Yet those walls weren't shelter—they were my chains,
Binding me tighter, increasing my pain.

Eventually, I knew I could no longer pretend,
Living alone wasn't something to defend.
So here I am, telling you what's real,
I'm hurting, I'm struggling, but I want to heal.

Perhaps I've felt lonely because I've shut you out,
Ignored your knocking, wrapped myself in doubt.
But today, I'm ready to change what I see,
By showing you my heart, my door's key.

"HOME IS WHERE THE HEART IS"

December 1, 2024

Blending whimsy with poignant symbolism, this piece transforms an anatomical heart into a cozy home, complete with windows, shutters, and a warmly lit door. The vibrant red and pink tones breathe life into the structure, while the bright blue arteries curve upward like chimneys, evoking both function and fantasy.

Each detail, from the glowing windowpanes to the rustic wooden door, reinforces the concept of the heart as a sanctuary. This illustration beautifully captures the idea that home is not merely a place but an emotional anchor, where love and connection reside.

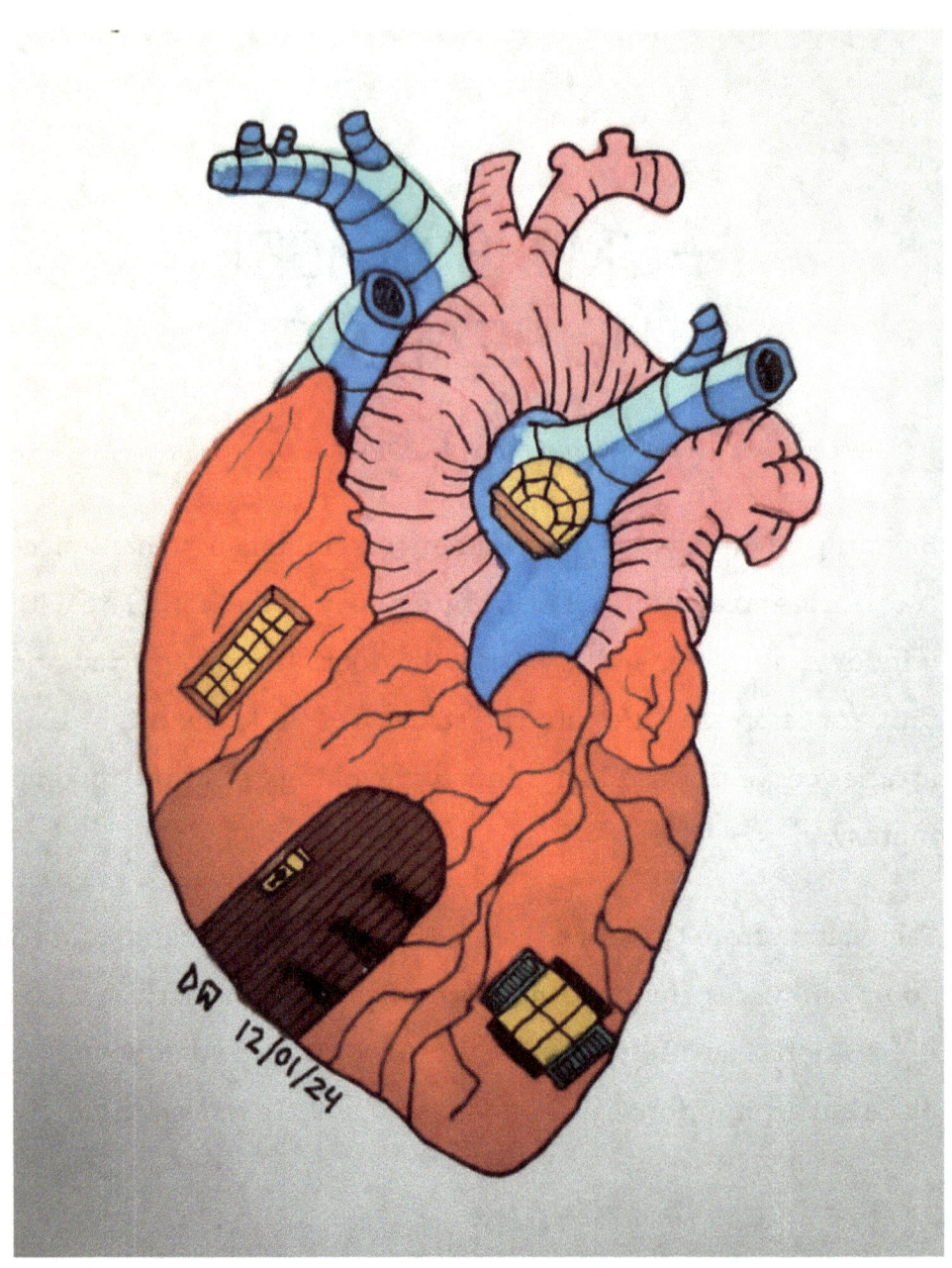

HOODED FIGURE

Everyone talks as if they understand,
As if depression's a concept they can hold in their hands.
But depression is a hooded figure, shrouded in gray,
Standing just outside, waiting to stay.

It's the sight of blood dripping red from your skin,
And thinking, "How beautiful," as darkness sets in.
"They always said red was my color," you muse,
A sick little thought that you didn't choose.

It's lying in bed for hours untold,
Salt tracks on your face, your body grown cold.
Tracing patterns in paint on a ceiling so still,
Accepting this life as a bitter pill.

It's a hole in your chest that swallows your breath,
And calling it life while yearning for death.
Not as an end, but a sweet, soft reprieve,
From pain you've accepted, a burden you grieve.

It's poetry carved on the surface of skin,
Publishing scars where no one's let in.
Cutting your ankles, not wrists, out of fear,
Desperate to be seen, yet no one comes near.

It's writing "alone" and seeing "home,"
Turning pain into gifts that are yours to own.
Admitting to paper the thoughts you won't share,
Hoping for healing but finding despair.

It's hearing your mother through walls far too thin,
Calling you addict, disappointment, and sin.
Telling you sadness is not your right,
That your tears are a weakness, a pitiful sight.

It's sitting alone as laughter rings clear,
Family so close, yet you can't feel near.
Learning too young that love can betray,
That family's not always love on display.

It's wishing to shatter your heart into shards,
And toss them to the waves like forgotten cards.
It's feeling like shoes that never quite fit,
Like life itself is a joke you don't get.

It's seeing the happy as copies, the same,
Smiles in magazines that put yours to shame.
It's packaging laughter in tiny little piles,
Wishing the worthy could borrow your smiles.

It's viewing your past as a film you don't own,
For claiming that pain would mean you've outgrown
The hope that tomorrow could still be alive,
Instead of succumbing to thoughts that deprive.

It's a hooded figure, persistent and grim,
Standing outside as the light grows dim.
If you shut the door, it pounds even more,
Obsessive and cruel, it rattles the floor.

And when anger flares, you swing the door wide,
Screaming, "I'm scared!" to nothing outside.
But the words come out as a soft, broken plea,
A whisper that trembles and falls to your knees.

"ROCK THE DRAGON"

June 30, 2024

 This dynamic piece merges strength and mysticism in a vivid display of power and resolve. A fierce warrior, adorned in traditional garb and painted face markings, stands tall, wielding a wooden staff as flames roar at his feet. Behind him looms an imposing green dragon, its scales gleaming and fiery red eyes radiating intensity, evoking an aura of ancient, untamed energy. The interplay between the warrior and the dragon symbolizes a connection of courage and control, a balance between human resilience and mythical ferocity.

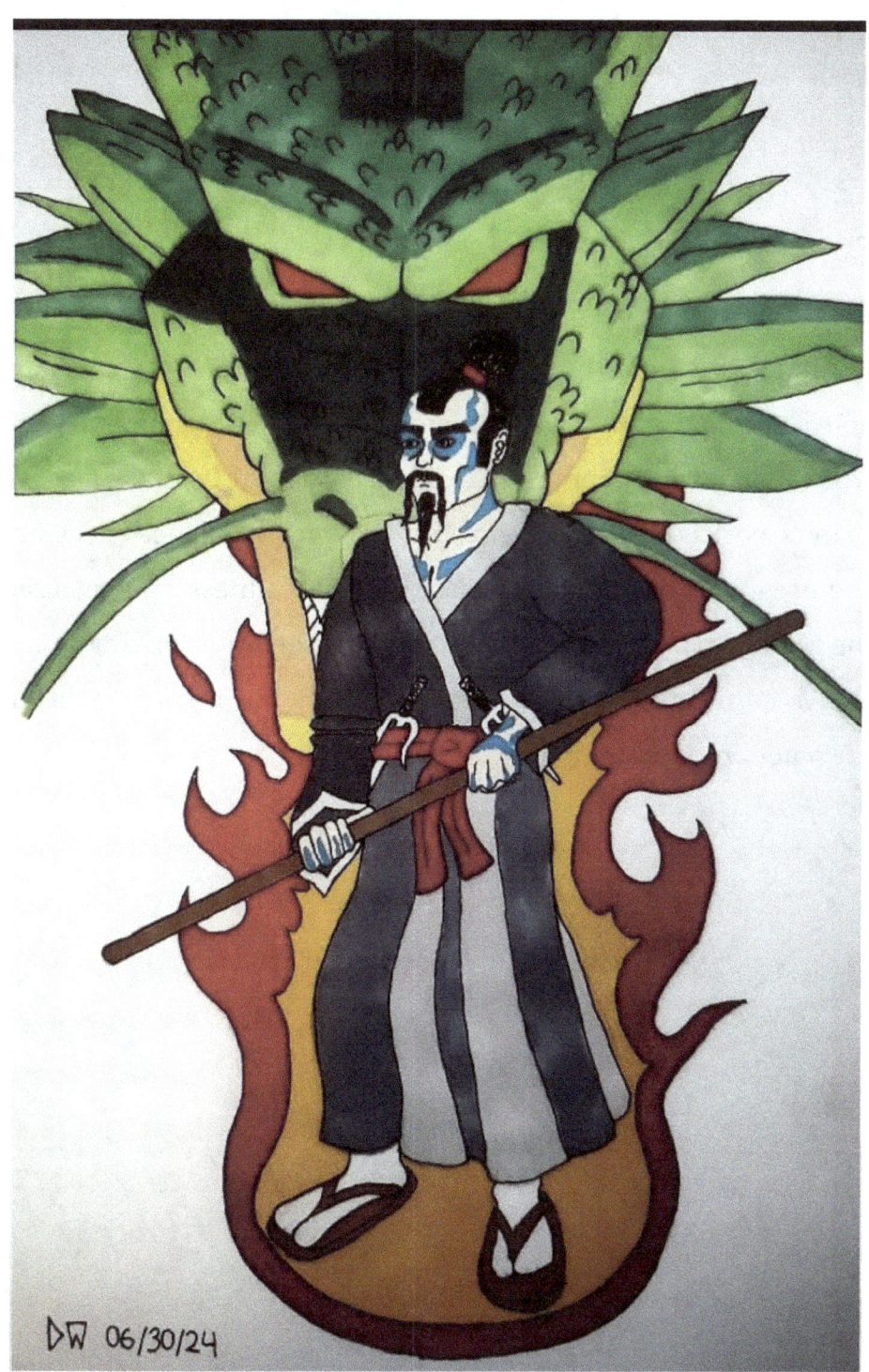

ABOUT THE AUTHOR

Kiana Jimenez is a writer, poet, and advocate. As the creator of *Poetic Bipolar Mind*, she shares her reflections, poems, and stories, exploring themes of resilience, mental health, and love. Kiana's work is deeply influenced by her personal experiences, and she uses her voice to destigmatize mental illness and celebrate the strength of the human spirit. When she's not writing, Kiana enjoys connecting with readers and drawing inspiration from life's quiet moments.

Follow her journey at:
Blog: Poetic Bipolar Mind
Instagram: @poeticbipolarmind

GALLERY OF WORKS BY DAVID WHITE

David White's art explores themes of emotion, growth, fantasy, and surrealism. Below is a curated list of his works featured under *Dave White Illustrations*.

Featured Works in This Book:

Distant Planet – October 1, 2024

Sell Yourself – July 1, 2024

Blank Canvas – July 8, 2024

Serenity – May 9, 2024

Pieces – May 18, 2024

Lotus – November 5, 2024

Self-Growth – September 15, 2024

FACEFEAR – May 19, 2024

Demolition – September 7, 2024

302 – August 31, 2024

Psychedelic Sunflower – August 18, 2024

Stop & Go – August 24, 2024

Cruising – September 7, 2024

The Ghoul – May 9, 2024

Ghostship – July 1, 2024

Fantasy Nightscape – June 8, 2024

Time Crunch – September 20, 2024

Rock the Dragon – June 30, 2024

Black Rose – December 1, 2024

The All Knowing – September 17, 2024

Home Is Where the Heart Is – December 1, 2024

Find these and other incredible works by David White at:

Instagram: @davewhiteillustrations

Website: https://davewhiteillustrations.wordpress.com/

For custom illustrations or inquiries, visit: https://poeticbipolarmind.com/the-art-barn/

AUTHOR'S NOTE

This book has been a labor of love, reflection, and growth. It's a testament to the power of art and words to heal, to connect, and to transform. Each piece holds a fragment of my journey—my struggles, triumphs, and everything in between. My hope is that this book offers solace to those who need it, understanding to those who seek it, and light to those who feel lost. Thank you for taking this journey with me.

RESOURCES AND SUPPORT

If you or someone you know is struggling with mental health, please don't hesitate to seek help.

Below are resources that can provide support:
National Suicide Prevention Lifeline:
1-800-273-TALK (1-800-273-8255)
Crisis Text Line:
Text HOME to 741741
NAMI (National Alliance on Mental Illness):
nami.org

You are never alone.

www.ingramcontent.com/pod-product-compliance
Lightning Source LLC
Chambersburg PA
CBHW071055240526
45469CB00006BD/2316